T0162310

Yoga the Sacred Science
volume two

SADHANA
The Path to Enlightenment

Yoga the Sacred Science
volume two

Swami Rama

Himalayan Institute Hospital Trust
Swami Ram Nagar, P.O. Jolly Grant
Dehradun - 248016, Uttarakhand, India

Acknowledgments

We would like to express our appreciation to Connie Gage for designing the cover, to Wesley Van Linda for the many services rendered in producing this book, and to Kamal for book design and production. We would like to especially thank Anne Glazier for meticulously checking the Sanskrit in the manuscript and her thoughtful help in generating the glossary. Last, but not least, we would like to thank Dr. Barbara Bova for compiling and editing this extremely valuable edition to the works of Sri Swami Rama.

Editing: Barbara Bova
Cover design: Connie Gage
Second printing 2017

©2011 Himalayan Institute Hospital Trust

ISBN 978-81-88157-68-6
Library of Congress Control Number: 2011937867

Published by:
 Himalayan Institute Hospital Trust
Swami Ram Nagar, P.O. Jolly Grant
Dehradun - 248016, Uttarakhand, India
Tel: 91-135-247-1233, Fax: 91-135-247-1122
src@hihtindia.org; www.hihtindia.org

ALL RIGHTS RESERVED. No part of this book may be reproduced in any form or by any electronic or mechanical means including information storage and retrieval systems without permission in writing from the publisher, except by a reviewer who may quote brief passages in a review.

Table of Contents

Foreword

Whether you are a long-time traveler of the path of yoga or you are just preparing to undertake the ultimate journey within, you will find this second volume of *Yoga the Sacred Science* to be an indispensable companion. Other requisites according to Swami Rama are simple and few: you, as you are, not as you pretend to be; a solid relationship with the guru within, your conscience; discipline and sincerity; faith, determination and inner strength; a cheerful, positive mind; a healthy body and a clean, quiet environment; and, most important, a fierce and unremitting desire for enlightenment. You might also want to simplify your life and dispose of a lot of irrelevant baggage now.

The introduction has been excerpted from an article by Swami Rama presented to the International Conference of Scientists and Religious Leaders on Shaping the Future of Mankind, at Kyoto, Japan, July 17-22, 1978.[1] Though it is in a different, more formal style from the rest of the text, it has been included because it concisely conveys Swami Rama's passionate feelings about religion and science and their relationship to spirituality. It also provides the rationale for the main body of the manuscript, as

---

1   Swami Rama, *Inspired Thoughts of Swami Rama,* (Honesdale, Pennsylvania: Himalayan Institute Press, 1983), 171.

proclaimed by Swamiji: "Cease this incessant talk about God and seek to meet and know God personally."

The greater part of the main text of the book has come from Swamiji's lectures on the Yoga Sutras of Patanjali, presented at the Glenview Himalayan Institute in 1977, and other early lectures and writings of the 70's. This was the time of the spiritual revolution in the West. We were ready for change, for new meaning and purpose to our lives. Swami Rama had left his beloved master and the Himalayas to come to America to teach and to selflessly share his indisputable knowledge of one of the most profound sciences and philosophies known to humanity. He literally blew our minds with his seemingly miraculous feats of mindbody control, and with the basics of pure yoga and meditation he unlocked previously sealed and unfathomed doors. His teachings and demonstrations of yogic accomplishments broadened our perspectives and changed our lives forever. There was no room for doubt. Spirituality was just what we needed, craved and had been waiting for to complete our lives. It seemed too good to be true, and it still does, as his loving guidance remains in our hearts and his teachings and writings continue to remind us to go within, to seek within.

It is those same teachings, largely based on the philosophy of yoga as described by Patanjali in his Yoga Sutras, that are reproduced here for everyone to share and explore at his or her own pace and level of understanding. These teachings embody a range of infinite possibilities of interpretation and experience. This volume focuses on the practical aspects of the path to enlightenment as declared in Sadhana Pada, the second pada of the Yoga Sutras and the foundation of spiritual practice in yoga.

Any errors in the manuscript belong to the editor who humbly apologizes.

Now tread the path of pure yoga to pure knowledge.

Barbara Bova
16 August 2011
Himalayan Institute Hospital Trust
Jolly Grant, Dehradun, India

Introduction

We read in the Bhagavad Gita that human intelligence operates on three levels. On the lowest level it sees a part of something and considers that to be the whole. On a higher level it gathers many parts and tries to create the whole by joining the parts together. At the highest level it sees the whole first, and thereby comprehends all of its parts. This last is the level of pure intelligence.

Ever since human intelligence became aware of itself, it has tried to understand its own nature and the nature of the universe. From the earliest human beings to modern humanity the same questions have recurred:

Who am I?

What is this universe?

What is my relationship with the universe?

Are these realities beyond the reach of my understanding?

The earliest seekers did not pattern their inquiries according to any particular religion, science or spiritual path. Although these three disciplines differ in perspective, they are interrelated and have all played very important

1

roles in humankind's quest for knowledge of the basis of life. When we state that we believe that someone else had an unnamed experience, we are following a religion. When we are primarily concerned with the nature of the universe apart from our intelligence, it becomes science. And when the experience of inner reality is personal, it is spiritual. The early spiritual leaders were the first scientists. They discovered that the scientific principles that govern the universe are not entirely separate from the principles that govern the mind. It is thus that the spiritual traditions of the ancient past gave birth to many sciences. For example, yogis long ago developed the most advanced principles of arithmetic and geometric models simply by experiencing the patterns that brain waves create. When these patterns are projected out from the mind, they become points, lines and triangles. The yogis sent their minds probing into the intricate energy or pranic patterns of their own personalities and not only came up with energy maps of the body but also discovered the basis of anatomy. The ancient yogis did not develop a highly complex technology in modern terms because their contribution to humanity was in a different direction. It is now well known that yogis are capable of demonstrating in experimental situations many phenomena that continue to baffle the scientists of today.

The founders of scientific inquiry in western civilization were the great philosophers of Greece, who inquired both into the nature of intelligence and the nonintelligent universe. Monks were the first astronomers and surgeons, and for centuries, sciences such as mathematics, astronomy and medicine were preserved in the monasteries of all religions. The Arab founders of western medicine, like Ibn Sina (Avicenna), found no conflict between discussing the nature of angels on one hand and establishing medical colleges on the other.

Although they did not deny the importance of understanding the external reality of the universe, the early seekers realized that it was not possible to understand the nature of the universe and the world of matter without first exploring the depths of inner consciousness. When they probed into the depths of their own consciousness they discovered that all consciousness is one and permeates the universe. The great philosophers, prophets and saints from all cultures and religions, the adepts, the enlightened and the liberated have resounded this truth throughout the millennia. For example, the Vedas declare: *I am the first-born son of eternal truth.* Similarly we read in the Upanishads: *As though lightning flashed; such is the moment when the great Brahman (the Absolute One) becomes known.* Krishna showed the cosmic expanse of the great consciousness to Arjuna on the battlefield of Kurukshetra. Lao Tze, the Buddha and the founders of other great systems of philosophy inspired their disciples by conveying a similar truth. Other sages like Socrates and the *rishis* of the Upanishads have all declared that the infinite is the source of the finite. They proclaimed that the One and the many are not opponents, rather, the many dwell within the One. From the potentialities of the One emanates the magic show of the world of *maya,* destined to ultimately return to infinity in the One. The whole universe dwells within a single unitary point of consciousness from which it evolves and to which it returns. The Upanishads state: *There are no diversities in the universe; all is a single infinite expanse known as Brahman.* Science studies the evolution of the multiple universe and observes the many and their interrelationships; spirituality seeks to experience the innermost one. There is only one gold, but there are many ornaments made of gold. Gold does not become many by changing its name, shape or form.

The prophets of the Old Testament repeatedly testified to hearing and seeing God's voice and vision. Those prophets spoke in such powerful words it was obvious they were speaking from oceanic depths far beyond the shallow surface of intelligence that ordinary human beings explore. Believers are often asked how they can rationally accept the words of the masters to be true. But how can we not accept something when many witnesses in all parts of the world at different times have testified to the same reality in similar words? Were they all insane? Was the Buddha insane to sit absolutely still for forty-nine days to reach enlightenment? Can any insane person sit still for even forty-nine seconds? The words of Christ have been reverberating around this planet for the past two thousand years. Why not the words of all the billions of others who called themselves sane? The power behind the words of the founders of religions came from a reservoir that is present in everyone and can be verified only by probing deep into one's own intelligence and consciousness.

Fundamentally all the great religions teach one and the same thing and lead to one place. However in the West religions are based mainly on external teachings, whereas the spiritual traditions of the East lead to the center of consciousness within and deal with real experience rather than concepts about it.

All the religions of the world have essential and nonessential aspects. The difference lies in nonessentials, not in essentials or fundamental truths. The essential, eternal aspect that is fundamental to all religions is divine truth. Truth existed before religion and humanity existed. Truth existed before, exists now and when the entire cosmos goes to its final annihilation, truth will continue to exist. Truth was there before Christ, Krishna and Buddha were born. These great people didn't create anything new; they were only messengers of truth. They changed the basket according to the times, but the teachings were the same: *There is only one existence. If truth is everywhere, there is no place for untruth.* Once someone asked Mother Theresa, "Do you believe in evil?"

She replied, "I don't have time to think about evil. I remember the Lord all the time with mind, action and speech, so how can I believe in evil?"

Unfortunately many disciples who were blessed to hear the words of their masters firsthand did not always understand them. Sometimes they tried to comprehend the masters' words by guesswork, without themselves going deep enough into the experience of contemplation and meditation. Through this guesswork they interpreted the words of the masters in various ways, thus causing disagreements. This resulted in many systems of belief that became the different religions of the world. Within these systems of belief arose the nonessential aspects, which vary according to religion. In this way the paths of religion became separated from true spirituality.

Problems arise when members of a religious community don't understand the essential part and try to follow only the nonessential part that declares, "I am Christian, I am Jewish, I am this, I am that," and determines which garb you should wear. Sometimes you decide to exchange each other's garb, thinking that will help you. But no one jacket can suit all.

When people get caught up in the nonessential aspects of religions, they become fanatical and divided. As long as religions divide us, all of humanity cannot be united under one roof. Even though persons of different religions may meet, they are not able to fully exchange and share their experiences for they remain within the limitations of the nonessentials and the boundaries of fanaticism. The nonessential aspects of religions tell you what to do and what not to do, eliminating the need to think about who you are or what your purpose in life is; you should just believe in and depend on God. The theories of religionists do not satisfy intellectuals or logicians.

Everywhere in the realm of religion I have encountered locked doors. If ever one door chanced to open, I was disappointed by what lay behind it. I am not saying you should be irreligious; rather, you should be beyond religion. You should not love another person because that person was born in a certain family or is of a certain religion; you should love others because they are human beings, no matter who they are, no matter from which country they have come or how intelligent they are. If you put boundaries around yourself, you will always remain individual. Be free from your religion and you will find that there is something beyond the nonessential aspects. There is no need to be fanatical. There are many avenues of approach, but there is only one truth. Truth is a principle that should be brought into practice in daily life. To understand truth it is not necessary to follow any particular religion. You simply have to be a student of life. The great sages received that wisdom from the center of consciousness within.

Religion may be necessary in the preliminary stage but it surely does not allow one to be one with the whole. It is like a moth that eats Kashmir wool to prove to other moths that Kashmir exists. God's existence does not depend on our proofs. There is something wrong with the philosophers and theologians for they have the curious notion that God is a kind of hypothesis that can be analyzed and discussed.

You talk of meeting God without actually knowing what God is or understanding why you want to meet God. You usually cannot adjust yourself to live in harmony with a human being who is similar to yourself. With all the weaknesses that you have, you cannot live peacefully with one person and yet you say you want to live with God, without understanding what that means. It is like searching for a mirage and wasting your time and energies. If you talk or think of God, an image of a church, a temple or a human being may come to you. Whatever you have considered to be the most perfect and ideal being, that image comes to mind when you think of God. You try to understand God with your individual mind and its boundaries, but you cannot go beyond that, because the human mind has difficulty conceiving of anything higher than a human being. You may imagine wings on a human being, a kind of half-bird and half-human being, and call it an angel; or you invent something very frightening and say it is the devil. The mind can wander within a given range, but it cannot really visualize anything greater than what you are. The mind only has the capacity to understand the names and forms of the world; it cannot penetrate the subtler aspects of your being nor understand the life force itself. The finest image you have of God is your own image, and your mind cannot conceive of anything beyond that. You search for God without understanding what it is, so your search remains unfulfilled. This is not the way to develop. God to me is a real annihilating fire and indescribable grace. I accept both.

Religion and science may disagree, but science and spirituality cannot disagree because both are experiential. Science explains the nature of the *non-I*, that which we do not identify with. But no scientist can explain to you from where you are receiving life. Scientists have much more to learn from yoga than yogis do from science.

In order to understand fully the relationship between science and spirituality, we need to know how the unity and multiplicity of the universe are intertwined. All the energies that flow in the universe, whether in a single human cell, within an atomic particle, in the gigantic distant suns or in the vast masses of gases from which multitudinous galaxies are yet to be formed, are all interrelated. If the energy of even a single atomic particle were lost, the whole structure of the principles on which the universe is built would crumble and vanish. Every physicist knows that worldly objects exist and operate on many levels of reality at once, as though these many were occupying the same space and time and presenting to our poor, limited senses a display of mutually exclusive and contradictory facets of existence all at once. The ancient Jain philosophers thought of light as atomic; others viewed it as energy. Today we know that light is both a vibration and a photon, depending on how we view it. Thus the earlier efforts of science to define everything as a one-level reality have met with abysmal failure. Those who have unraveled the secrets of the world of spirituality have also stated that each level of reality has its own internally valid and self-consistent laws of existence and operation.

Though the physical sciences declare these principles on an intellectual level, they can only state the facts as observed. They cannot create a state of consciousness or convey the feeling of unity to human intelligence. When a mind is trained only to deal with the multiples, it will take much unlearning and purification to develop an intuitive grasp of the unity that is infinity. As it is true that the spiritual inquiries of the ancients led to the discoveries of science, it has also been said that scientific inquiry can lead to spiritual seeking. The scientist explores the object; the spiritual seeker sees the glory.

We hear today's astronomers and physicists proclaim repeatedly that what seems to them like a mystery play of the physical universe must have a metaphysical author. They guess it to be so but do not know for certain.

A very ancient dialogue occurs in the Vedas:

> *"Believe in God, if indeed He is, but where is He? Who has seen Him?"*

> *"Open your eyes and see. Right here before you I am shining in my full glory in every object you behold."*

Modern humanity's dilemma then is this: Science focuses on facts and says not to believe without the facts; religion insists you believe without understanding. Religions, which are supposed to help mankind, try to keep their followers bound with regulations and external observances. Who will then show the path of truth and freedom—the freedom of moral choice and the freedom from blind obedience?

The future of humanity must be seen from both ends. On one end are the means for physical comfort, nourishment and health of the body, transportation, communications and our insatiable curiosity about every atomic particle in every galaxy. On the other end is the very nature of man, independent of the physical universe. What can a person accomplish without tools? Though he can explore outer space, can he dive into the spaces within? Can the scientist control his irritation, anger and frustration? Can he lengthen the duration of his breath to accomplish the dream of a long life? Can he, without any medicines or injections, merely by using the controls of volition, stop his heartbeat or place himself in suspended animation? Can he bring about a peaceful state of mind among the citizens of the world without the use of pills or physiological manipulation? To all these questions the answer is no. Nor can spiritual seekers bring nourishment to hungry stomachs without the help of agricultural scientists. To repeat a cliché: Without science, humanity is crippled; without spirituality, it is blind.

Even if you have everything—children, a home, financial stability and career satisfaction—still you are not happy. The reason is you have not touched the center of happiness within you. The experience of the center of happiness comes through spirituality. Religious practices can help you to become spiritual, but it is in spirituality that you become conscious of the reality—God within and God outside. In spirituality all resources are directed toward your subtler levels directly, and then to the Lord. But in religions all practices are devoted to an external God without tapping the source. It is not possible to know the Cosmic Self without knowing yourself. By knowing yourself you will know the Self of all.

Science is also an experience of spiritual intelligence, but in relationship to the external universe. Some of the basic laws taught by both scientists and spiritual traditions are common. Without understanding these cosmic laws, we would fail to perceive the true relationship between the two facets of reality. For example, take Newton's third law of motion: *For every action there is an equal and opposite reaction.* On the spiritual path, the same becomes the law of karma: *For every action, there is a reaction.* The wording is different, but the principle is the same. By applying our understanding of Newton's law we row our boats or pilot our jet planes. Through an understanding of the karmic principle we know that what we do to others is actually a seed being sown in our own minds in the form of subtle impressions, which will ripen later for us to reap. We need to emphasize that the principles of science can be applied to spirituality, as the universe is an emanation of the divine intelligence. Scientific thought first occurs in the human mind where a spark of divine intelligence is already active. If science had no basis in spirituality, the intuitive flashes of scientific principles that often occur to true seekers of knowledge would not take place. All knowledge arises from deep within the principle of the intelligence of consciousness.

We must trace the intellectual processes on which science depends to their very origin, intuitive knowledge. We must acknowledge that intuition, too, diversifies itself into intellectual processes that return again to their spiritual homeland in states of deep contemplation and meditation. If depending on science alone, humanity will become so attached to the physical objects, that insatiable curiosity combined with unsatisfied greed will lead to our destruction in a very short time. Even now thousands of living species are becoming extinct, and beautiful rainforests are being converted into deserts. The spiritual ways of life of many ancient cultures have been disturbed and irretrievably lost. The time has come for humanity to turn its curiosity inward and put its trust in spirituality so the higher intelligence will prevail. When this happens, needs, but not greed, will be fulfilled, and the present restlessness of masses upon masses of minds poisoning the collective unconscious of this planet will cease its agitations. Guided by pure consciousness, science will serve humanity, while spirituality itself will help to raise human relationships to a highly unselfish level of fulfillment.

This is no empty promise. It can be so. This prophecy can be fulfilled. Let science return to its holistic origins; let the scientist remember that it was not for nothing that the monk was the first astronomer and surgeon. To the people of religions we have to say: Abandon the verbosity of your theologies and preaching from the pulpit. Return yourself and your followers to the origins of spirituality, the inner conscious experience of dwelling in the infinite light that is God. Cease this incessant talk about God and seek to meet and know God personally.

No matter which culture, religion, or philosophical background we come from, we all have one and the same purpose of life, and that is to get freedom from all fears and pains, to attain that state of wisdom called perennial happiness, everlasting bliss or peace.

The Whole Process of YOGA Is an Ascent into the Purity of Absolute PERFECTION, Which Is the Original State of Human Beings

The yoga tradition considers science and spirituality to be two parts of a complete whole, as they are both primarily experiences within the principle of intelligence. Here we are not talking of an intellectual inquiry or philosophical speculation because these are founded on guesswork. Thousands of philosophers have already created many encyclopedic works based on such speculation without inner experience. Because they could not agree among themselves, their writings merely produce confusion and conflict among their readers and followers. Their language primarily relates to external realities and cannot convey the vastness of the dimension of intelligence that the founders of spirituality have experienced. While the founders of true spirituality agree on the nature of their inner experience, philosophers continue to disagree until eventually, in rare cases like Socrates and Kant, speculation gives way for transcendental silence to flow through. The same applies to the speculative theologian who ventures elaborate and complicated guesswork as to the true meaning of the words spoken by the founders of the spiritual traditions. Quite often such guesswork has been falsely given the name of contemplation, without realizing that true contemplation is a silent experience.

Neither the philosopher nor the theologian has any business pretending to proclaim a truth till he has come face to face with the deeper nature of intelligence where consciousness goes far beyond the triangle of space, time and causation.

Those on the path of yoga are often mistaken as being in the same class as various religions, churches, sects and cults whose believers, not the ancient founders, are incapable of scientifically demonstrating the truth of their beliefs. Yoga is not part of any religion nor is it merely a system of exercises to keep the body fit or to cure minor physical disorders. Yoga is a scientific approach to life that provides a discipline for the fullest development of the soul, mind and body. Yoga teachings have been handed down in India through a living master-discipleship tradition that has preserved the authenticity of the practices and ensured the survival of the yoga tradition. The practices of yoga science help you to understand yourself; only then can you understand your religion, the universe and other beings. The whole process of yoga is an ascent into the purity of absolute perfection, which is the original state of human beings.

Yoga deals with the experiential aspects of man's liberation from human imperfection and suffering, and is concerned with practical methods for attaining this state, using the philosophical doctrines of Samkhya as their basis. Samkhya philosophy supports the philosophy of yoga — *samyak akhyate*, that which explains the whole. The Samkhya school of philosophy admits of two ultimate realities: *purusha,* or cosmic consciousness, and *prakriti,* or elemental matter. The manifest universe evolves out of prakriti. It results from the coming together of purusha and prakriti, matter being permeated by consciousness.

What is more, this scheme of evolution applies both to the macrocosm (the universe) and to the microcosm (a human being). Yoga bases its teachings on this scheme of evolution in the microcosm. It concerns itself with the practical aspects of involution or the return from identification with the manifest body and mind to ultimate consciousness.

Yoga teaches you how to be and gives something that religion does not provide. Yoga is an exact science that helps you to know yourself on all levels—body, breath, mind and spirit. From your childhood onward your education has led you to examine and verify things in the external world, which is constantly changing. Your education has not helped you to become aware that there is another reality within that never changes. You have to learn to accommodate and understand both realities and the whole structure of life, including the known and the unknown, the apparent and the real. In the Yoga Sutras, Patanjali emphasizes the importance of understanding life within, while not ignoring the external world. According to Patanjali, the prime goal of human life is to establish oneself in one's essential nature.

Yoga science asserts that the human mind is not established in its true nature because it identifies with the objects of the external world. The purpose of yoga science is to lead you within to the highest state of tranquility, wisdom and bliss, in which you remain fully conscious and aware of the reality. Yoga teaches you how to see within. If you remain an outsider, your mind will continue to be scattered and you will not understand why you have come to this world, what the goal of life is or how you should relate to others. You do not know yourself, yet you are trying to know others. In order to know and understand yourself on all dimensions, you will have to search within. Once you understand and know yourself, you will be able to analyze the entire universe and your relationship with the universe and with other beings. By analyzing a drop of water, you can know the ocean; by analyzing this human life, you can know the whole universe. The same Self that dwells within you dwells in everyone. That Self is the center of consciousness.

The term *yoga* is derived from the Sanskrit root *yuj* (to yoke or join). In yoga philosophy *yoga* means "to unite with the Universal Self." Your prime duty as a human being is to know yourself and then to know the Self of all. For that, you will have to train yourself. Others can inspire and help you, but self-training requires effort. No matter how powerful are the instruments or other means that you have, those means cannot help you to know the reality within. Even the finest telescope through which you can see the stars and planets clearly, cannot help you to know your internal states. You don't have to go anywhere to train yourself because every walk of life presents an opportunity to learn. You don't need drugs, a guru or any other external help. But you need guidance in how to practise and how to conduct your life so you can attain happiness in this lifetime, here and now. As a human being you have all the knowledge within, but you have to make effort to come in touch with that knowledge. Human effort is called ascending power.

When you have exhausted all effort and used all the resources you have, finally the power of the Lord will touch you. That is descending power, or grace. You cannot get enlightened without grace. There are four types of grace: grace of God, grace of the scriptures, grace of a teacher who loves you selflessly and grace of yourself.

If you have the first three graces but do not have your own grace, the others are of no use. To have your own grace means to remain constantly aware of the reality within. When you go within and come to understand the resources therein, many mysteries will reveal themselves to you. When you understand and rely on that which is within, nothing will be impossible. The absolute truth will radiate through you.

Before you make any effort to go inward to the source of light, life and wisdom, you have to have an understanding of the external world, and that is not so easy. It is difficult to collect accurate data from the ever-changing external world. In addition, the experiences gained through the senses cannot be considered valid because the senses are limited. Another obstacle is that the mind, which tends to be dissipated rather than one-pointed or concentrated, commits mistakes when it collects data. Therefore it is essential that you first train your mind and senses.

Patanjali's Yoga Sutras consist of four *padas* (literally "feet," here "sections or chapters.") In Samadhi Pada, the first of the four padas, Patanjali has explained that the key point for first-class students is to have control over mind and its modifications. You have to systematically understand mind and its modifications in order to recognize which of the various faculties and modifications of mind are untrained and thus not helpful to you. For example, whenever you want to do something, *manas,* the lower function of the mind, questions: *Shall I do it or not? Buddhi* is the higher faculty that tells you: *If you do it, this will happen; if you don't do it, this will not happen.* If you do not train the buddhi, you will lack decisiveness, judgment and discrimination. By having control over mind and its modifications, you can attain *samadhi* (union), a state of perfect equilibrium and tranquility.

The second pada, Sadhana Pada, is the foundation of spiritual practice in yoga. Many methods are given in Sadhana Pada to help you practise and become free of all the *kleshas* (afflictions), so that you can control your mind and modifications and realize the Self. This pada is for those who are not yet fully prepared: *I want to know my mind. I understand that my mind and its modifications are not under my control and so they create obstacles for me. I do not know my true nature or how to enlighten myself. Please introduce me to those gems of truth that will help me begin to practise.* Such persons can also attain samadhi.

Patanjali begins the second pada with specific instructions: "Now, you have to be very practical. You have learned enough philosophy and you have been speculating too much. Now, start to tread the path." Next he explains various methods to tread the path and introduces the very preliminary, though also very important and practical, aspects of yoga. Many of you will mistakenly think this chapter is not meant for you because of the word *preliminary*. Although you may think you already know many things, that kind of knowledge has very little to do with the real knowledge of something. And even though you say you know something, it doesn't necessarily mean you have assimilated it. For example, you know you should not tell lies, yet you continue to do so.

The secret to knowing is this: To know something means just to know it, without creating any resistance. Your thoughts should go through the filtration of buddhi and other aspects of *antahkarana,* your inner instrument, before you communicate with or talk to someone. And when you listen, just open your heart and listen, so that you clearly understand what you are hearing. Learn to listen with your heart, not with your mind.

Traditionally the teacher of the Yoga Sutras begins with the explanation of the first four aphorisms of the first pada and then moves ahead to the second pada in order to explain how to do *sadhana* (spiritual practice). Initially you might be hesitant to do sadhana because you are afraid it will be too difficult and you don't understand what it is. As a result, without having tried, you decide sadhana is not necessary for you and you don't want to do it. It's true that it's not easy to live in the world and do sadhana. You have many responsibilities with your family and career and cannot always do what you want, but still you have to try. It seems difficult only if you don't make any effort; all things become easy when you practise. Practice is different from theory. If you do something again and again, you will find that your body and mind quickly adjust to it.

When you start to practise, it is important not to impose extreme rules on yourself. Be patient and gentle with yourself. Don't become disappointed with yourself or say you cannot improve or tread the path of enlightenment. Never give up your practice. Practice is valid and will reveal to you all the mysteries hidden within. Then it will become easy for you to shape and guide your whole life toward your goal.

Some people seemingly have come in touch all of a sudden with the higher potentials within, and a complete transformation of their whole personality has taken place. But in reality this could happen only when a person is on the path. The process of self-transformation is a gradual process that cannot be completed overnight. On the way to Damascus Paul came in touch with the higher potentials within. He was going to Damascus because he had not found satisfaction in what he was doing. After having searched everywhere, finally he chose to follow the path to Damascus, and on the way Self-realization dawned. Self-realization comes only when you are fully prepared. Never stop working with yourself. If you prepare and discipline yourself, you can definitely attain that which is deep within you.

Even though the world has very little to offer in comparison to truth, still the world is very powerful. You are so attracted to the world and all its charms and temptations; imagine how truth will attract you if you are on the path of truth. When you begin to search for truth and you practise, you will experience, and that experience will guide you. The path of spirituality is not devoid of pitfalls. It can lead you to an egotistical way of life if you misunderstand what it is. You may think to be spiritual means to withdraw yourself from your duties and responsibilities and become overly conceited. Spirituality is *adhyatma,* that which comes under the domain of the center of consciousness within. Actually, there is nothing to attain. Spirituality means to be constantly aware of the absolute reality. All sadhana is meant to purify the mind and make the mind one-pointed and inward so it can be directed toward the center of consciousness that dwells within the inner chamber of your being. Physical growth is in the hands of nature; mental growth and spiritual growth are in your hands. The second chapter is completely devoted to sadhana and is replete with methods of practice to help you improve yourself by learning to control your mind and its modifications. Then, you can attain a state of samadhi and realize the Self within.

I have found that without the knowledge of truth there is some hunger in me to know and know and know. No matter how much I have known, I have not felt satisfied. The more I wanted to know, the more I studied. And the more I studied, the more unsatisfied I felt. This means I have still to know truth. The day I know truth, perhaps this hankering will subside.

PRACTISE Systematically, Step by Step

Patanjali begins the second pada with a very practical method that helps to gain control of the mind and its modifications. He has beautifully described it: *tapas svadhyaya ishvara pranidhana kriya yogah.* Here he is introducing kriya yoga, which encompasses three basic principles: *tapas,* control of the senses; *svadhyaya,* study of the self; and *ishvara pranidhana,* surrender to the Lord within.

Kriya yoga, or preliminary yoga, is practical yoga. Since it is not possible to immediately gain control of the mind and its thinking process, your emotional life, and all your desires and appetites of the primitive fountains, you will have to practise systematically, step by step. The first step is tapas. *Tapas* means, "to know how to control the senses." If you do not have control of the senses, the data the senses collect from the external world will not be clear, and the mind will not be able to decide, judge or function properly. Throughout the Yoga Sutras, Patanjali repeatedly stresses the importance of understanding the nature of the senses and how they dissipate the power of the mind by distracting the mind from the purpose of life and drawing it outward to the charms and temptations of the external world. Now, you have to train your mind not to follow the senses but instead to go within to the deeper levels of your being. When you know how to control and guide the senses, the objects of the senses will no longer have the power to sway you. Then you will be able to perceive the true nature of the objects of the world; you will better understand the nature of your mind and will be able to concentrate the energy of your mind and channel that energy inward. Tapas means to control the senses so they do not dissipate the energy of the mind.

Svadhyaya means "self-study," which is the study of one's nature, including one's actions, thoughts, emotions and desires. Without svadhyaya and self-awareness you cannot understand your actions or behavior. In your current state of mind you do not know why you move the way you move, why you think the way you think, why you speak the way you speak or why you act the way you act. Even though you are not aware of it, you do not make a single gesture or movement without mental effort. Although some of your actions and gestures are conscious, most of them are unconscious. For instance, sometimes you behave badly and later on you repent. You know you have acted foolishly and that you should not have behaved in such a manner, but you do not know why you did it. Before you do anything you should be aware of what you are going to do and of all the consequences of doing it. Then, if you still want to do it and are prepared to accept the consequences, go ahead.

When you start to tread the path and begin to study your internal states, you may find it very difficult because you have never faced yourself as you really are. It's easy to criticize others and see what is not good in them, but you prefer not to know your own imperfections because of a strong ego or sense of *I-ness*. Even though you may want to improve, you are afraid to know your own weaknesses. You think it isn't possible for you to improve, so you go along with the current wave of knowing everything that appears to be fascinating. You are not aware that the faculty of mind that wants to know everything in the external world can also lead you to that height where you can know the reality. If you have not known the reality, it is of no use to know anything else. It is like collecting junk and putting it in the basement — you are just creating more problems for yourself. Those who remain on the thinking level do not get the opportunity to see what they are within. You are not as small as you think you are. There are many other glorious and wonderful levels within you. When you understand your thinking process and can go beyond it to the unconscious mind, you will discover that the world within is far superior to the external world. Svadhyaya will help you to encounter both the superficial complexes and the deeper potentials within you. Without self-study, enlightenment is not possible.

Ishvara pranidhana (self-surrender) is one of the highest ways to live and leads to the height of Self-realization. In the city of life there is someone sleeping who is called Ishvara, or purusha, the center of consciousness from where consciousness flows on various degrees and grades. *Isha* means "the one who directly controls your life." Your whole being belongs to this center of consciousness. Whatever you find here, there and everywhere, within and without, is governed by the great power called God, or Ishvara, who dwells within you. Because of ego you do not know this center is within you. Ego is helpful in that it makes you aware of your own body and your own self, and helps you to know what is you and what is not you. But ego is not interested in the law of life that there is one unity in diversity. Ego claims to be the proprietor of the body, when actually it is only a representative of the reality. It creates a wall between you and the reality, the center of consciousness within. This separation from the reality is the root cause of all misery.

The body can be compared to a workshop. In that workshop ego claims to be the proprietor, mind is the manager and the senses are the workers. In this arrangement ego is aware of two things: *I* and *mine*. This is false identification. The proprietor of this whole property is the center of consciousness. You have to make ego aware that there is someone higher who is the real proprietor.

Because of your lack of awareness of the center of consciousness within, whatever you do is actually for the satisfaction of your ego. All your acts of worship and the so-called loves and attachments in your life are just for your ego. In order to help yourself you will have to surrender your mere self or ego before the real Self, the Lord within you. This does not mean you have to renounce your ego. Self-surrender does not mean you should surrender your real Self before the world or anyone else. Rather you have to surrender the self that is imitating the proprietor before the reality. You have to let ego become aware of the reality. As long as ego is not aware of another existence that is higher than it, it will continue to grow stronger and stronger. Ego can become a means for enlightenment only if you make it aware that it is only a representative of the reality.

There is only one power within and without that governs you and the universe, and that power is Isha, or purusha (pure consciousness). Purusha is sleeping in the city of life, deeply seated in the tomb of the body, like a hidden jewel in a coalmine. Purusha is not at all affected by this world. One of the Upanishads beautifully explains it:

> *In the tree of life there are two birds. One is eating the fruits of the tree of life; sometimes it is enjoying but at other times it is suffering and weeping. The other bird is only witnessing and is not affected.*

It is the ego that is enjoying the fruits. You keep trying to satisfy the ego again and again. Ego keeps saying, "This is mine and this is mine. This is all me. I am everything. This body is mine and the senses and mind are mine. All the objects of the world are mine for sensual pleasure." That is why ego continues to suffer.

Purusha is only witnessing and therefore does not suffer. Purusha is not involved in what is going on in the world, though it seems to be. Suppose you place one hundred transparent glass jars, full of water, outside on a sunny day. When you look into the jars, it appears that the sun is inside the jars, but it is not actually there. The sun is not at all involved with the jars. One who is suffering on account of ignorance sees a hundred suns inside the jars, but purusha does not. One who has attained the highest reality understands the differentiation between the seer and the seen, or the object and the one that is witnessing the object. For the one who has attained, it is immaterial whether the object is there or not. But those who have not attained will continue to suffer as long as they have a feeling of individualization and identify with the objects of the world. You will have to make sincere efforts and go through certain spiritual disciplines if you want to become aware of that force within you. You will have to dig down deep, and your face may get dirty in the process.

In many of the great *mantras* there is one word, *namaha*, which means, "O Lord! Nothing belongs to me; everything belongs to thee." With this wisdom you can live in the world and enjoy every breath of life. Till now you have been living in a state of confusion. You study the Yoga Sutras and decide you want to be a yogi. Therefore you think you should no longer eat food, drink or make love. In essence you think you should not live. Patanjali does not say that everyone should become a monk. Whether you want to become a monk or you want to remain in worldly life, if you practise these three principles in your daily life, they will help you. Always remember the first aphorism of the second pada: *tapas svadhyaya ishvara pranidhana.*

You Have to Become MINDFUL of the KLESHAS

The purpose of the practice of kriya yoga is to remove the kleshas. The kleshas are the cause of *duhkham* (pain, worry, misery and suffering). They hinder your progress and prevent you from attaining samadhi. Patanjali says in order to understand the philosophy of the kleshas you have to understand the four basic principles of yoga:

There is pain and misery.

There is a cause of pain and misery.

There are ways and means to get freedom from pain.

There is a state that is free from all pains.

Buddhism borrowed these ideas from yoga science and teaches the same thing. Buddha was born as a prince in a Hindu family. He had all possible worldly means: a beautiful wife, a palace, a big kingdom, a strong and healthy body, and he was a very handsome man like Christ. He left his home when he became aware there was suffering in the world.

In the practice of kriya yoga, first you should acknowledge there is pain and that you suffer on account of pain. You cannot ignore pain or pretend there is no misery or pain. Every human being feels pain, and sometimes the cause of the pain is unknown. Pain can come from external sources or from one's own physical, mental or spiritual limitations. For instance, you may have the desire to attain the highest truth, but when you find you are not able to attain it you become depressed.

The word *klesha* is often misinterpreted to mean "evil, devil or sin" because of common belief in these notions. Patanjali says those who propagate these ideas do so in order to keep people under their control, just as a horse rider uses a stick and his heels to guide a horse on the right track. Those persons who are not educated and do not want to or do not have the capacity to understand, can be controlled by the suggestive power of such ideas as the devil and sin. For them, the terror and fear associated with these things are helpful.

In reality there is no need to worry about going to heaven or hell. You create your own personal heaven and hell, and demons are also self-made. The devil is a sickness of the mind as are so many physiological diseases, which can be controlled by mental focus. Nothing can be more injurious than the human mind for it is capable of creating disasters of the highest magnitude. The capacity of the human mind to create an atom bomb and drop it to destroy a whole country is evidence of the destructive potential of the human mind.

Literal interpretations of the concepts of the devil and sin are not for an educated person who is looking for answers to the vital questions of life:

Who am I?

From where have I come?

Why have I come?

What is the purpose of my life?

Where am I going?

If religious books, scriptures, or teachers cannot satisfactorily explain these vital questions or give you the answers, you have to look elsewhere. Try to explore your origin and understand what you are, how and why you have come to this world and what the purpose of your life is. In this way you will gradually become aware of the higher dimensions of life and you will question more:

What is the source of knowledge?

From where can I receive this knowledge?

What are those obstacles that come in the way and prevent me from having clarity of mind and the knowledge that can help me to attain the highest state of freedom from misery?

If you study the Book of Psalms, or the Sermon on the Mount, you will not find any mention of sin. These scriptures are meant for those who have more understanding and have started to question life. In the Sermon on the Mount Christ did not say you would go to hell if you committed sins. Instead he said: "You are like a child. You have all the potentials and if you continue to grow, you will become like your Father. You and your Father are one."

Although the major religious traditions of the world talk about sin, there is confusion about what sin actually is. No one is a sinner, but you frequently commit mistakes and thus create many obstacles for yourself.

In desperation you pray to the Lord for help. You may feel inspired when you pray, but otherwise you remain ignorant. For example, if you decide you are no longer going to work, you may spend the whole day praying to God to give you food. If someone comes and takes pity on you, you think God has answered your prayers. But actually God has not sent you any food. Someone gave you the food because they felt pity on you. Patanjali says to be realistic and not to create obstacles for yourself. Even if you cannot have control over your mind and its thinking process, you can try to have control over your actions and speech. You can make effort to stop saying what you don't want to say and stop doing those things that are not helpful. Patanjali describes those things that are not helpful for you as kleshas, or obstacles. You have to become mindful of the kleshas.

Patanjali clarifies this concept by explaining the five categories of kleshas: *avidya* (ignorance, or lack of awareness of the reality); *asmita* (sense of egoism); *raga* (attachment toward the things of the world); *dvesha* (repulsion); and *abhinivesha* (strong desire for life, or abject fear of death). These are the great afflictions, the causes of all misery. *Moksha* is final emancipation from all the kleshas and all pain and suffering.

There may be times you feel so happy and joyous that you think you are free from all pains and miseries and have fulfilled all your karmic duties. But there are *samskaras*, the subtle impressions of past actions, deeply hidden in the reservoir of the unconscious that can suddenly come forward to remind you that you are not yet free. They are stronger than the superficial events happening on the surface and they do not allow you to go forward. You may have decided the world is of no use to you and have renounced your home and family and joined a monastery. If you try to go back to the world, the world will kick you again and let you know there is no place for you in society. Even if you have accepted all of this, still those deep-rooted samskaras will come and disturb you again and again. The following story will demonstrate how this can happen:

Once there was a swami whose guru had asked him not to have anything to do with three things: gold, the charms and temptations of beautiful women, and name and fame. His master warned him these three things were very powerful, and told him if he could avoid them, enlightenment would definitely come. So he solemnly promised his master he would not be tempted. But he did not realize what a difficult task he had been given. As Swami Rama Tirtha, a great sage from the Himalayas, had said, "When I needed the world, name and fame and money, nothing came to me. But the day I renounced them, they started to follow me. Fortune is like a flirt. She runs away from him who runs after her and runs after him who runs away from her."

So the swami went on his way until he came to a river. He could see that a segment of the bank of the river had collapsed, revealing three golden vessels full of gold coins. He reminded himself of his master's orders and pondered the situation: *I am a swami so I don't need you. Why did you never come to me when I needed you? But now that you are here, I should make use of you anyway. With this gold I will build a temple with a big hall where people can assemble for satsang. Many swamis can come and teach there. This is something good, and since I am not doing it for myself, it is okay.*

Immediately he set out to get help for this project. He asked two contractors to come to the site where he had decided the temple should be built and he said to them, "I need your assistance. I am a swami so I cannot touch gold. I am requesting you to take this gold and build a temple on this site. Please ask the architect to come."

Not able to believe their good fortune, the contractors walked away from the swami and conspired to cheat him. One of them said, "No one cares for this swami. He has left the world so nobody will notice if he dies. Let us drown him in the river and then we can share this wealth."

The other contractor readily agreed. They walked back to the swami and before he could realize what was happening, they attacked him. Then they tied a big rock to his neck and threw him into the river. To relieve themselves of any guilt feelings they told each other he deserved that. And without any further concern, they happily walked away with all the gold.

Fortunately for that swami his master was closely looking after him. As soon as the contractors were out of sight, he appeared and cut the rope and pulled him from the river. Then he scolded him for not keeping his promise.

The swami protested that he had not gone against his word since he had not intended to use the gold for himself. His master told him he should not have gotten involved with the gold at all. And so the swami assured his master it would not happen again. After this incident, when anybody offered him money he would turn his face away and refuse it.

He returned to the forest, determined to continue his sadhana. A woman who was a widow saw that he was alone and took pity on him. She approached him and asked, "Sir, can I give you some milk from a distance?"

"Yes, as long as you don't come near me. Keep it over there."

From that day she started to bring him milk every day, gradually placing the milk closer and closer to the swami. The swami had confidence that she was a good person so he did not reproach her. Again one day she spoke to him, "Sir, how can you sit the whole day? It doesn't seem possible. I could never do that. Your legs must be paining you. Perhaps you would like me to press your legs?"

Without hesitation he agreed. After a few days she started to live with him, and when two people live together something is bound to happen. Their child arrived after some time. One day the swami was carrying the child on his shoulders, and the child urinated on him. A swami who was passing by saw what had happened and he shouted, "Hey! What's the matter, Swami? Is it the juice of the Gita that is flowing from your shoulders?"

This incident shocked him back to his senses and he said to the woman, "You have enough wealth to look after the child. Now let me go so I can complete my sadhana as I am not yet realized."

She knew he was determined and so did not try to prevent him from going. He left and went further into the deep forest, vowing to never again allow money or any woman to distract him from his sadhana. But his troubles were not over.

One day a villager came to him to ask for money for the marriage ceremony of his daughter. He pleaded with the swami to help him. In response the swami pulled out one hair from his beard, gave it to the man and said, "If you put this in a safe place, your supply of money will never be exhausted. But don't tell anyone about it or that I have given it to you."

Of course when the villager returned to his home he was so excited he could not refrain from telling his wife what had happened. Since the woman could not keep such exciting news in her heart, everybody eventually came to know about it. The story became known even in far away places. As a result many people came to him and pulled hairs out of his beard until his whole face was bleeding. This is how the swami came to be the victim of the third forbidden item, name and fame.

The inherent desire for name and fame was the immediate cause, but there were also deep-rooted samskaras. When this swami renounced his home and family, he did so under the illusion he would be free. Patanjali says a false renunciation is not the way to freedom. You cannot live perfectly until you remove the cause of all the kleshas that are deeply rooted in the unconscious. Without rooting out the cause, the effect of the cause will remain, and you will continue to reap the fruits of your actions. And until you understand the cause, you will not be able to help yourself. If you are performing a *karma* (an action) and do not know why you are doing that particular action, that karma will continue to motivate you to repeat it. You will be like a machine or robot, living a mindless life. If you chop down a tree, unless you remove all the roots of that tree, after some time many branches will again start to come out of the tree stump. Sometimes you may think you have conquered your internal states, but without rooting out all the causes, you will not be able to control your destiny.

Now you can understand the importance of the first aphorism of the second pada. In this aphorism Patanjali is expressing the significance of the practice of kriya yoga to help you remove the kleshas and to deal with the difficulties you will have to face in removing them. This is Sadhana Pada, so you have to be very practical now. There is no need to become a philosopher, but you have to be very clear. Even when you think you have completed your karma, there are certain kleshas of which you are not aware, and you will still have to deal with these latent kleshas that are deeply rooted in your unconscious. They will make their presence known to you. You may find that suddenly you are again being controlled or forced to do something that distracts your whole course of life and completely shatters you.

You cannot easily get rid of the kleshas because they are deeply intertwined with your karma. Even when you go from this world you will carry all the seeds of your karmas with you. Whenever the opportunity comes, again you will come forward and repeat the same karmas in another lifetime. Patanjali says by performing your karma skillfully and selflessly you can cross the mires of delusion and get freedom from the painful cycle of deaths and births. You have to be reborn again as long as you have desires or karma to fulfill. And desire always brings pain instead of joy, because all the joys of the world are mingled with pain.

Patanjali says the root cause of karma is in the kleshas. The kleshas arise from attachment to the body, which has its source in the union of purusha with prakriti. This attachment to the body is so strong that no matter how much pain you experience from this attachment, still you remain attached. Here, purusha refers to you, me and all other individual souls. I am not talking about purusha as pure consciousness. Your purusha is individual consciousness that sees and experiences through prakriti.

Purusha and prakriti are two forms of the same thing. Just as water can exist in three forms — vapour, solid and liquid — energy has two forms, energy itself and matter. Matter can be converted into energy, and energy can be converted into matter. The most superficial or dimmest aspect of pure consciousness is prakriti, which is nature or matter, while purusha is energy or consciousness. Each has a particular role to play. Instead of playing the role it was meant to play — to become aware of the center of pure consciousness — purusha has become caught up in a different role because it identifies with the objects of the world. Purusha should be able to see more clearly through prakriti but it does not because it remains in a condition of intoxication due to its union with prakriti. Purusha will be able to see the Absolute only when it learns not to identify with the objects of prakriti or the manifested world. This is the technique purusha has to understand. Then the question comes: Why did purusha and prakriti come together?

Purusha came in touch with prakriti for improvement for his own sake, or so he could see more and more. But instead of seeing more and more he got lost in the world and forgot the reality. That is why purusha suffers. There are two principles of life: the female principle and the male principle. Purusha's union with prakriti is the union of the male principle with the female principle. It is not easy to explain why these two want to come together, nor is it possible to convince the male and female they should not come together. It is simply their nature to identify with each other. Tantric literature is devoted to the study of the male and female principles and refers to these principles in the manifest world as Shiva and Shakti respectively. If you study tantric literature, you will understand why these two principles are needed in the manifest world.

Patanjali says by constant awareness of the reality you will get freedom from all the kleshas. There are ways of getting freedom from pains and miseries and there is a state that is free from all miseries. One of these ways is the practice of kriya yoga. The three principles of kriya yoga: tapas, svadhyaya, ishvara pranidhana—austerity, self-study and surrender to the Lord—will help you remove the five kleshas. Once you conquer your internal states you will attain the highest state of samadhi, the state of tranquility or pure consciousness that Patanjali describes. The nature of pure consciousness is freedom from pain and misery. It is not affected by the kleshas. However, when you practise you are certain to encounter the kleshas.

KNOW that You Do Not Know

Avidya means "ignorance, or lack of knowledge of the reality." *A* means "no," *vidya* means "knowledge." According to Patanjali, ignorance is the root cause of all pain, misery and suffering. You are suffering not because someone wants you to suffer, or because a devil or something evil is making you suffer, but because of lack of knowledge and clarity of mind. A preliminary step on the path of enlightenment is to accept the premise that you are ignorant — to know that you do not know.

Apart from its general significance, avidya includes the following: the delusive attitude of regarding transitory things as everlasting, such as conducting oneself as if one's youth would last forever and one's beauty would never fade; unwarranted acquisition of material luxuries as if one's wealth would never be exhausted; the belief that happiness lies in the indulgence of carnal pleasures; and the incapacity to discriminate between that which is pure and impure, or between right and wrong.

Another meaning of avidya is the failure to perceive the true nature of the objects of the world, to see them as they are. You don't see the universe as it really is because your perception of the universe is individual. You see things only partially through the little windows of your eyes. This partial knowledge has nothing to do with the totality of experience and thus cannot be considered to be truth. For example, it may appear to you that the horizon is very small. But it all depends from where you are seeing it. Suppose that currently you are seeing the horizon through a small window. If a great person comes along and takes you to the roof, you will see how vast the horizon really is. When you're flying in an airplane, things don't look the same as they do when you're on the ground. You don't see this apparent reality as it is when you're dreaming or when you go to deep sleep. Likewise you will never see what you consider to be reality when you experience samadhi. When you see things as they are, you neither hate nor love them, nor fear them; you just know them.

The term *maya* is closely related with avidya. Maya can be described as apparent reality — that which does not exist though it appears to exist. *Ma* means "no," *ya* means "that." An example of maya is a mirage in the desert. Even though you think you see it, it doesn't exist. Maya can cause you to have an accident, but it cannot enlighten you. Maya is the reason you see the one absolute truth as many. You can better understand the relationship among the individual soul, maya and the Absolute by the following analogy: Suppose a thick layer of ice covers the ocean, and on the layer of ice there are trillions of holes. All the individuals and creatures of the universe can be represented by the holes, the sheet of ice is maya, and the ocean that lies beneath symbolises the absolute reality. When the sheet of ice melts, maya disappears along with all the holes and all individuality; the reality alone remains. Avidya and maya are the same, but avidya is individual and maya is cosmic. Maya is only an instrument that Brahman uses to project the universe. Through maya Brahman projects Himself as many.

Once my master gave me a practical example to help me to understand what maya is:

When I lived in the mountains with my master, I used to teach the scriptures. My favorite scripture was *Panchadashi*, one of the books of Vedanta. But when I would teach the topic of maya, I would feel sad because I didn't understand it. One day I said to my master, "Please give me a practical example. I know what maya is theoretically, but I don't really understand what it is."

He smiled and said, "Tomorrow I will show you what maya is."

I became very excited and thought, *When I know what maya is, I will be free from its clutches and then I will meet the Absolute.*

The next morning, as we were returning from our bath in the Ganges, my master stopped all of a sudden and wrapped himself tightly around the trunk of a tree.

I asked, "What is this? Why are you doing such a strange thing today?"

He replied, "I'm not doing anything. It is maya that has done this to me. Will you please help me?"

Even though I was young and very strong and tried my best to pull his legs away from the trunk and to release his hands and arms, I was not successful. Finally I asked him to release his hands.

"I cannot, because this is maya," he insisted.

When he could see that I was working so hard to release him that I was beginning to sweat, he asked, "Are you tired of trying to release me from the bondage of maya?"

"Yes," I said.

"Now, I have decided to release myself."

And he simply released his arms and legs from the trunk of the tree.

You can remain in the bondage of avidya or you can release yourself. It is your choice. You are the way you are because you wanted to be this way. No one else has decided for you or made any plans for you. This is your own planning and it will go on till eternity if you do not have any goal toward which you direct all your energy. Each individual creates avidya. Thus it is your own ignorance and superimpositions that are responsible for your suffering. You may think that God has created this ignorance, but if this were true, He would also be responsible for giving freedom from ignorance. You alone are liable for your manifestation and entanglement in your thoughts, actions, speech and desires. You are ignorant because your knowledge is very shallow. You think the world is real and you live in the world with the misconception that all you see is truth; you consider that which is noneternal to be eternal. Your vision is blurred because you have become intoxicated by the charms and temptations of the external world. If you don't train your mind, it will remain in this state of ignorance and delusion, a state in which you don't have knowledge of the cause of ignorance, how to eliminate the cause or how to attain that state which is free from misery.

According to our philosophy God is not the creator of this world. If you believe God created this world, it means you believe in two existences: In the beginning God and some matter were there; with the help of that matter, God created this world. But who created that matter? If God were omnipresent, omnipotent and omniscient, why would he need matter to create the world? If such were the case, it would mean that He was dependent on that material, which would have had to simultaneously exist with the power called God. There would have had to be dual, Self-existent entities—God and the material with which He had supposedly built this world. Scientifically speaking, two realities cannot exist, because existence is only one. No matter where you go, there is only one Self-existent reality. That Self-existent reality was never born, will never die, is always present and does not need anyone's support or assistance.

It is written in the Vedas, the most ancient scriptures, that the absolute reality manifested itself into many. This is all the manifestation of God. I will explain to you how the very existence of this universe is only one. Suppose there is a dot. Now that dot expands and is called one. This one will always remain one. Two means twice one; three means three times one; ten means ten times one. Nothing has happened to one. If you reduce one from ten, the existence of ten will be lost. It will become nine. If the one that exists is taken out, we will no longer exist.

Then how did this expansion come? How are there so many forms and so much variety? If I have a seed in my palm, there is a tree inside this seed, with leaves, and flowers and fruits that have seeds inside. Each small seed contains within itself the potential of millions of seeds. When you sow a seed, you know that the seed will grow and produce many more seeds. Likewise, one Self-existent seed has manifested the universe and that is how we are here. Only that One has the power to manifest. God did not create the world; One manifested into many.

There cannot be two gods because God dwells everywhere. There is no space for Him to move. Usually, you apply your small mind to the task of knowing God, and when that small mind fails, you say God does not exist. Even without your acknowledgment, God is everywhere. If one tiny little bit of you remembers God, nothing will happen to Him, and you will not become the jewel of God's crown. God has never asked you to believe in Him. Similarly if you don't believe in the sun, the sun will still shine for you. Even if you deny one hundred times that the sun exists, nothing is going to happen to the sun. If you don't believe in a breeze, even then you will get fresh air. Your belief does not make any difference. God exists. If you are ever in a situation where no one can help you, you will find that faith will come to help you. I am not trying to convince you to have faith or to remove reason within. I have seen it happen:

There was one swami who was very intellectual. He was more scholarly than I and could speak many languages. If I would make a statement about something, he would immediately come up with some logical point and dismiss the idea. I stayed with him for several days. Whenever I would say something about God he would use logic to convince me there was no God. Though I did not know God, I could feel there was something. He asked me if I was an atheist. I replied, "No. I believe that God exists."

He instantly opposed me, "This is all fantasy. Man has created the image of God for his own convenience. Actually there is nothing like God."

So I said to him, "Swamiji, do you know there are beautiful valleys of flowers deep in the Himalayan Mountains?"

"Really? You are from the mountains? You are not lying to me?"

I answered, "No, I am speaking the truth."

I decided to take this opportunity to examine the power of God. It had now become a matter of prestige for me. So I persuaded that swami to come with me into the mountains. We had only a small tent with us. It began to snow heavily and I took the risk of going by a road where I knew there would be no chance of coming back. It took three days for us to travel thirty-five miles.

Wherever I went I would always take time to sit down to meditate because my master had told me it was very useful. I thought, *Why should he lie to me? A person lies when he has some selfish motive. I am his child and he would never hurt me. I should follow his good suggestions.* So when the time came for me to sit down to meditate, that swami became upset.

"Hey, come on. Why are you closing your eyes? Can't you see how heavily it is snowing?"

I proceeded to meditate in spite of his protests. By the time I had finished, the depth of the snow had gone beyond thirteen feet and our tent was buried inside the snow. He was in a state of panic because he was having difficulty breathing. I told him, "Swamiji, if you say God exists, the snow will stop; if you don't say it, the snow will continue, and you will die. I believe in God, so I am not going to die."

At first he resisted. I told him to just do it as an experiment. I repeated, "Say, 'O Lord, you exist and I am very sorry for my ignorance.' All you have to do is say this and it will stop snowing."

Because of his fear he agreed, "For the sake of experiment only, I will say it."

I was very familiar with mountain climate and I knew the signs that indicated that the snow was about to stop.

He cried, "O Lord! Help me! Let the snow stop."

And the snow stopped.

I said, "The snow has stopped, but how can we walk back thirty-five miles with the road so deeply covered with snow? It seems there is no way out."

Again he panicked, "What shall I do?"

I answered, "Just meditate!"

And he started to sing the praises of the Lord.

The question arises, if this is all God, who is omnipresent, omnipotent and omniscient, then where do you exist? You are a citizen of several worlds—waking, dreaming and sleeping—but actually you are the dweller of the fourth state, *turiya;* your existence is in fact the same as the existence of the absolute reality. You are not aware you have all the powers within yourself, so you have no faith in yourself. If you don't have faith in yourself, how can you have faith in God? Deep down within you there is a center called the kingdom of God. You simply have to go within to experience that center of silence. It is very easy to say that God exists somewhere far away and to think you are small and good for nothing. As a *sadhaka* (one who is following a spiritual path) you have to understand that whomever you call God, or absolute truth or reality, does not dwell somewhere far away from you, but is within you. Be conscious of this truth.

For me truth is God. I am not talking about relative truth; I am talking about the truth that was never born and will never die, that is omnipresent and omniscient. If truth is universal how is it possible for you to be excluded from the highest truth that is everywhere? It means He is in you and you are in Him. Then where are you? Your existence is not your existence. Who can separate God and say a little bit of God is in Swami Rama, and a large bit of God is in the universe? If God is everywhere, He is in you and me also with full majesty. The moment you realize the absolute truth that is not subject to change, death and decay is within you, you will attain freedom from all fear and bondage. You have to have this confidence. This is called reasoned faith. Where is God? He is within. Where are you? You are in God, and God is in you. When you have this confidence, you will have no fears. If you really believe in God and you are in search of God, look into the deeper states of your being. God is there. This means you are a living shrine. You should look after this shrine knowing that it is the Lord's shrine.

In spite of having this confidence, still you want to know more and try to analyze where He is within you. Even within yourself, you have created divisions. One by one, if you reduce your limbs, you can still continue to live. But you cannot live without the breath, heart and brain. Of these three, God lives more in the heart, and you can reach there through the breath. The heart is the center that holds your being. This is not the physical heart that can be dissected by a surgeon's knife. In this context the heart refers to the center of the life force within you. It is beyond body, breath, senses and mind. This concept may be hard to fathom, as it doesn't seem possible for such a great majesty to live in such a small heart. But that's the beauty of it. That great majesty lives in the greatest and in the smallest both. If you can attain that state where you don't have consciousness of body, breath, senses or mind, you will be there. First understand and realize God within, and then you will believe.

When you dive deep and understand the whole mystery, you will experience that you are God and therefore not subordinate to any power. If you feel that you and God are different, this is an insult to the Lord who is the inner dweller and who is everywhere. If you are not God, then who are you? If you could separate yourself from the one reality, it would mean you were more powerful than that reality. There is only one who experiences and that one is called *Atman*. Atman is within you and you are Atman. Thou art That.

The world is like a dream. Just as dreaming reality is true for the span of the dream, waking reality is limited to a certain period of time. We can say this world exists, but it is not Self-existent because its existence is dependent on the existence of something else. Similarly a tree's existence lies dormant in the seed; it has no existence of its own. This is a great controversy — which came first, cause or effect? The answer is they both came together. The tree was living inside the seed; it came out because it was already there. This whole universe has come out from nothingness. If something comes out of nothing, it means it is nothing. Time and space have a cause. The final cause is the absolute reality or truth, which is Self-existent and so does not need any cause. That which is not Self-existent cannot be called truth.

Now means that which is eternal. There is only one thing that is eternal and that is truth. There was truth in the past; there is truth now; there will be truth in the future. To be in the now means to always be conscious of truth.

There are three definitions of truth: Truth is that which is not subject to change, death and decomposition; that which was never born so never dies; and that which is Self-existent and never needs support from anyone or anything. Truth never needs any evidence or proof. This world is full of names and forms that are continuously undergoing change. When the form of something changes, the name also changes. If you make a table out of wood, you no longer call it wood; now you call it a table. That which changes its name and form is not truth. Whatever you see in the world is subject to change, death and decay. Therefore, the world is not real. That which changes cannot be called real; that which is unreal cannot come from truth.

Within the human being is a center of light that infinitely surpasses the light of the sun, moon and stars. It has intelligence, brilliance and the power to discriminate. Because of this light, you can see other lights. You think you are seeing through your eyes, but actually the eyes are only gates. When you close your eyes, all things vanish. All the senses function because of the light within you. You cannot find that light by searching for it with your eyes closed. If I were to tell you to open your eyes so you could see the light, still you would insist there was no light because you are confused. As long as you continue to blindfold yourself, you will remain in the darkness of ignorance. One who is accustomed to darkness is afraid of light. You are afraid of the Lord because you are habituated to living in the darkness of ignorance. Darkness is the distance you create from the center of light. Darkness has no existence of its own; it is simply lack of light. There can be no compromise between darkness and light. Darkness can give you only darkness; light can give you only light.

Although avidya has no existence of its own, it dissipates your energy and prevents you from establishing yourself in the center of consciousness. Avidya has many faces. It is like a beautiful person who is hidden by a veil covered with glitter and multi-colored stars. You are so distracted by the glitter, it doesn't occur to you to look underneath the veil where the real stars lie.

You can remove the veil of avidya by sharpening the buddhi, the faculty of mind that helps you to distinguish between what is truth and not truth, what is eternal and not eternal. Those who are aware of truth are considered to be great persons; those who are not aware of truth are ignorant. For an ignorant person, the eternal and noneternal are deeply intertwined. In order to separate them the mind has to become one-pointed and penetrative, like a bee that collects fragrance from the flowers and converts it into honey. This is possible through meditation. As long as you are not enlightened, you will remain in the clutches of maya. You can fearlessly cross the mire of delusion that maya creates only with the help of pure knowledge.

In order to understand the pure knowledge that Patanjali is referring to here it is important to first clarify that there are many levels of knowledge and many steps in the quest for pure knowledge. For example, suppose I am thirsty and I have knowledge of water. When I stand on the mountaintop, from there I can see the river flowing; I have knowledge of the river, but that doesn't quench my thirst. So I go down to the foot of the mountain where I have a clearer vision of the river. As I walk toward the river I gain more knowledge, and when I reach the river I can see very clearly what a river is. But only when I drink the water is my thirst quenched. That is direct or experiential knowledge. Without experiential knowledge you cannot truly understand anything.

Jnana means "knowledge," *vijnana* is "the method to receive knowledge." Though there are many ways to receive knowledge, basically knowledge comes from three sources: sense perception, mental conceptualization and intuition, the infinite library that is far beyond senses, mind, ego and intellect.

When you hear, see, smell, taste or touch something, you are acquiring knowledge from external sources through sense perception. The knowledge that comes through sense perception is not sufficient to be complete knowledge, because the senses are very limited. When you see things with limitation, you are not seeing them as they are. The world looks the way it does to you because of your senses. If you had never used one of the senses, for example the eyes, your experience of the world would be different. Since everyone has similar senses, we all have comparable experiences. If everyone were to develop a sixth sense, the world would look different to you.

With the knowledge you receive through the senses you conceptualize and come to certain conclusions. You use this knowledge to function and express yourself in the external world. But the senses and the mind are not valid sources of knowledge. As long as you use the senses to collect facts and then ask the mind to know what they are, you are only in the first stage of knowledge.

This is knowledge through the mind. It is related to the past. You have known something from information you have gathered through sense perception and mental analysis. When you depend on knowledge acquired through the mind only you are living on one dimension and making use of very little of the total power of the mind. As there is no educational system that trains you to know and make use of the totality of the mind, the remainder of the totality remains submerged in the deep waters of your life. You train and educate only a very small part of the mind, the part that functions during the waking state. Consequently the thinking process guides all your actions.

There is another type of knowledge that comes through the buddhi, in which you know something through information gathered through your senses along with intellectual analysis. Buddhi is usually interpreted as "intellect" in English. There is however a difference between these two. Whereas the buddhi gives you the capacity to gain internal and external knowledge, the intellect is limited to knowing the facts with the help of the senses. You cannot depend on the intellect because it gathers data from the external world, which is subject to change. The intellect is like a small ruler with which the human mind tries to measure the vast universe.

The knowledge that is imparted in colleges and universities, the knowledge that comes from the environment and the knowledge that is instilled at home, are also not sufficient. Although the knowledge acquired through mind or intellect is shallow, you definitely need this knowledge to live in the world. But this information that you consider to be knowledge is superficial and will not help you to transform yourself or lead you to the inner world of Self-realization. Knowledge received through the mind is not helpful to fathom the deeper, subtler levels of your being. The purpose of mind is to function with the senses to understand the external world. Mind is not helpful to know the Self except when it has been trained to not disturb you. This is the purpose of sadhana.

One day you will come to realize that all the knowledge you think you have is in fact not yours. It is all just information. You gather so much information it becomes a burden for you. Because of the shallowness of the education you receive, your learning and your intelligence are limited to only one aspect of the totality of the learning process. As a result you know very little about yourself. You read what others have to say and form opinions based on their opinions. Much of the so-called learning process you go through is mere imitation. You imitate each other and think you are learning. That is not profound knowledge. Dark words can never give you light because light can never be a product of darkness.

You depend on the intellect so much you have forgotten there are other sources of knowledge, such as instinct. Instinctual knowledge is more apparent in the animal kingdom. Since nature governs the lives of animals completely, animals are much closer to nature. It is well known that before a natural calamity occurs, animals attempt to leave the area because they sense that something is going to happen. Human beings come to know only when it happens. The experts can tell you where earthquakes are most likely to occur, but they cannot predict when an earthquake is going to happen. Animals will leave a place if an earthquake is about to take place. As a result, very few animals die in an earthquake except for those who are sick or disabled. How is it that animals can know while human beings with so many resources cannot know? Human beings also have the capacity for instinctual knowledge. For instance a mother may suddenly feel pain and uneasiness and have the feeling that her only child who is far away is suffering. She comes to know later that her instincts were correct. I have had similar experiences:

I was very naughty in my childhood and it was so difficult for my master to control me at times he had to spank me. Even when I was twenty-one years of age I still troubled him. One day I decided to go out in the car. He said to me, "Don't go anywhere. You have to stay here now. Sit down."

"No. I want to go and I am going," I said defiantly.

"If you go, you will meet with an accident and I will be troubled."

I did not listen to him even though I also felt something was going to happen. I took the car anyway. I was driving so fast and recklessly that I lost control of the car and ran into a thick wall. Although I was protected from serious injury, it took two mechanics three hours to remove me from the wrecked car.

We both knew it was going to happen. That is instinctual knowledge. We all have that instrument within, but we usually choose to ignore our feelings and don't use it.

Although such experiences are not uncommon, for all practical purposes you have lost touch with nature because of your artificially acquired knowledge and intelligence. In fact this has happened to such an extent that now you require external means to see things. You cannot directly see or perceive things because the cultivation of instinctual knowledge has not been part of your education. You have gone so far with artificial knowledge that you cannot understand or feel what nature is any more. You don't like to walk barefoot on the ground or touch anything without gloves. You cannot see without glasses. You are disconnected from the finer laws of life and nature because your mind has become preoccupied with the comforts and means you think you can apply to help you to attain wisdom. You have no motivation to be sensitive toward that knowledge which will help you to get freedom from misery and pain.

Instinctual knowledge is definitely higher than intellectual knowledge, but each has its limitations. When you train your intellect through the acquisition of facts, slowly the intellect becomes more incisive and wants to understand more: *I am not only this body; body is just a part of me. I also have senses and a mind, but there is another part that is not known to me.* When intellect calms down, awareness takes over.

Awareness is a vague term, but it is important to understand it. Awareness is entirely different from knowledge. The difference between intellectual knowledge and awareness is this: For the knowledge you acquire with the help of the intellect you have to trust and depend on the world of facts; for awareness you don't need any support or help from cognition or the external world. For example, when you are alone in the darkness and can't see yourself, you don't need any external light or anyone else to know that you exist; you simply are aware of it. When you are inside a room, you are aware of the walls of the room. If you want to be aware of something more, you will have to go out of the room. When you say you are aware of yourself, it doesn't mean you are aware of higher consciousness. Similarly, you are not a realized person just because you say you are aware of the reality.

In order to be aware of the reality, you will have to attain the goal of life. Belief in God is completely different from the experience of the presence of God at every moment. My master told me that *sat*, *chit* and *ananda* (truth, consciousness and bliss) are three aspects of the Lord, the absolute truth. It is not necessary to run here and there to attain that state. A human being is the greatest of all shrines and the moment he comes to know this truth, he is free. To believe in God, or truth, is a mere belief; to realize that the Lord of life is within you is wisdom. Then you have attained something.

It is essential to make effort to expand your awareness. One way to do this is to study the scriptures and the experiences of great sages. But there comes a time when such study is also no longer needed, as a swami I met on the bank of the Ganges informed me:

I was sitting on the banks of the Ganges, reading the Gita, one of the great texts that imparts knowledge, when a swami came along and asked, "What are you doing?"

I replied that I was reading the Gita. He said, "Then you must still be a fool!"

I was so shocked at what he had just said that I just stared at him. Then I asked him to explain himself, and he replied, "The Gita is for those who still have conflicts. Arjuna had a conflict, and Krishna helped him to resolve that conflict. I don't have any conflicts so I no longer need to study the Gita."

I asked, "Are you sure you are not just boasting?"

"What do you mean? I am not boasting about anything. If you are not ignorant or in conflict, then why do you need to search for knowledge? If you are already full of knowledge, you don't require any more. Knowledge is eternal, Self-existent and here and now."

As your awareness gradually deepens, the power of the buddhi is also sharpened and you develop the capacity to discriminate between what is truth and what is not. Discrimination in the realm of facts is entirely different from discrimination between the eternal and noneternal. In order to develop this level of discrimination you have to have a clear understanding of both avidya and vidya. The buddhi, when properly trained, can lead you to a level where you understand not only what is right and not right, what is fact and not fact, but also what is truth and not truth. If you slowly work with your intellect and with the fire of discrimination, your intellect will shine like gold and you will attain a state of wisdom and awareness of the truth within.

Wisdom is not knowledge that you receive through mind; it is knowledge received through a vision. You will experience such visions when you have learned to have perfect control over your mind.

Emotion, which is more powerful than the thinking process, can also become a right source of knowledge, if properly directed. Emotion is one of the most powerful

resources you have. All great persons performed great
feats during a state of ecstasy, not through the knowledge
of mind. When your whole being spontaneously goes into
a state of tranquility through the experience of music, art
or something else that makes your mind one-pointed, you
are receiving knowledge through emotion. If you are in
love with somebody, your mind remains one-pointedly
focused on the object of your love. That is also considered
to be emotional knowledge. If you direct your emotions
toward one particular point, you can attain the height
of ecstasy. Many great sages of the world have attained
the highest knowledge through a state of ecstasy, where
mind does not function, intervene or reason. Mind is
not able to comprehend why it is happening. Among all
emotions the most powerful inborn emotion in humans is
sahaja bhava, the ultimate source of knowledge, intuition.
Intuitive knowledge is the finest of all knowledge and
does not need any evidence. The intuitive library within
is beyond sense perceptions and mind. It is very close to
the inner source of light, life and love. To be in touch with
the intuitive library, you have to quiet the mind. As long
as your mind continues to function, and you are disturbed
by mental argument, conflict or suppressed emotions,
such mental activity creates a barrier to the intuitive flow
and it is lost. Only when you relax the mind can the fund
of knowledge that is hidden beyond flow forward. The
first goal of sadhana is not enlightenment; the first goal
is to train the mind so it does not create obstacles for you.
Your initial effort should be to prevent the mind from
creating problems for you.

There is definitely something divine beyond this
phenomenal world. That divinity also dwells within
human beings. You come in touch with the finest of
knowledge from that divinity in you. It is not in the

body, breath or mind. It is beyond the mire of delusion created by your mind, in the silence within. When you experience perfect silence, the higher knowledge called intuition dawns from beyond all the superficial fields of consciousness and all the various aspects of the mind. Intuitive knowledge, like meditation, is beyond time. With the help of the practice of meditation, you can develop your intuitive capacity so that it becomes your real guide. Intuitive knowledge doesn't reveal itself bit by bit. When you touch the peak of divinity in the state of superconsciousness, intuitive knowledge spontaneously flows in leaps and bounds.

If you receive knowledge through the mind, you will always continue to doubt and search for evidence; you will always want someone to reassure you and confirm that you are doing the right thing. Once you come in touch with intuitive knowledge, there is no need for confirmation or evidence from any teacher, swami or yogi. You will know and know that you know.

Intuitive knowledge is unalloyed knowledge, the highest knowledge of all. The source of intuition is beyond the knowledge of the senses and the conscious and unconscious minds. It comes to you when your whole being attains a state of stillness. If you voluntarily learn to still yourself and attain a state of tranquility, nothing is impossible during that time. The fund of knowledge that is hidden beyond can flow forward and help you to solve a problem or to heal yourself or others. The knowledge that comes through the senses or through the mind is not perfect, but the knowledge that comes from beyond the mind, the finest of all knowledge, is pure knowledge. You have to prepare yourself to receive that impersonal knowledge by doing sadhana, just as you have to put gold in the fire in order for it to shine. When you go through tapas and the process of purification, Atman shines forth. You cannot see your face in a mirror if the mirror is covered with dust. If you clean the mirror, it will show you clearly what your face looks like. Spiritual practices lead to purity of mind. To truly understand any object in the world you need a one-pointed mind. Only a pure mind can attain that level of one-pointedness. You can know the extremely subtle Atman residing in the cave of the heart only through pure knowledge. Pure knowledge comes when you have acquired the knowledge of the scriptures from a guru who has been trained by his guru lineage. If you are so blessed to have such a guru, honor and serve him or her with humility and learn how to control your mind.

Mind is not a source of pure knowledge. As long as you use your senses to collect facts and then ask the mind to know what it is, that is inferior knowledge. When pure knowledge comes to you, it is entirely different. Nobody has created pure knowledge. It does not change in day-to-day life and cannot be modified. Whether it comes through the Christian Bible, the Vedas or any other source, pure knowledge is eternal because it comes from the Absolute. Absolute or pure knowledge is limitless, immortal and imperishable because it flows from the source of infinity. This knowledge is the source of all other types of knowledge. When absolute knowledge comes to you it will not be what you think of as knowledge. Pure knowledge does not come through the senses or mind. It reveals itself.

Between the crown chakra, sahasrara chakra, and ajna chakra, there is another chakra called *trikuti* in Sanskrit, located at the space between the two eyebrows, or *bhrikuti*. This is the guru chakra, the seat of the guru within. *Guru* means "knowledge." By concentration on the guru chakra you receive the pure knowledge that comes from the valley of intuition. A fountain can give you water to quench your thirst but the guru chakra is the only fountain that can give you the nectar that can make you immortal.

On both sides of this chakra there are two *sandhi* glands. When you master the technique of concentration on the sandhi glands, they form a sort of lens through which you can see far and beyond the range of normal vision. In effect, the vision becomes telescopic, both externally and internally.

The pure knowledge Patanjali is talking about is that knowledge that helps you to liberate yourself from ignorance so you can be free from all miseries and attain the highest state of consciousness. The knowledge that gives you freedom from all miseries cannot be partial knowledge. It must touch all the corners of your life and transform your entire personality. Transformation does not mean simple changes such as weight gain or loss, graying of hair or weakening of eyesight. The perfect knowledge that brings transformation is love. As a human being you have the capacity to experience pure knowledge because the infinite library of the highest of all knowledge, along with the source of infinite love, is already within you. Real transformation comes through awareness of the source of knowledge within.

A human being can be compared to a lamp that is covered with several shades. Though the light is there, it is very dim because of the many shades. As long as you remain in body consciousness, you cannot be aware of the reality that is hidden beneath all the shades. Intellectually you may know the light of truth is within you, but you are not aware of it. If you remove all the superimpositions that you have created one by one and go within to the center of consciousness, you will finally see the source of light, love and life, shining in all its glory. You will have to surrender the ego that lives in darkness before that light. That light is self-effulgent; it has not come from any other source nor has it borrowed light from any lamp or from the sun, moon or stars. The light that is responsible for understanding, seeing, hearing, touching, tasting or smelling comes from the Atman within, the source of pure knowledge. The whole universe is shining through that light. This means all the knowledge you have today, even that knowledge you have received though your mind, senses and intellect, has come from that same source of consciousness. Light and knowledge have no ideology; all religions are supported by the same light and knowledge.

Even though your true nature is happiness, you continue to create misery and suffering for yourself. As long as the lake of the mind remains disturbed, there can be no happiness. Nothing in the world can give you happiness. Amidst the great rush and roar of external progress, there is only darkness. You can be transformed only when you come to know that God dwells within you. Then your life will totally change and you will no longer feel your individual existence. You will know God exists and that you are a living shrine of God. If you remain aware of the reality, you will never be in darkness and there will be no place for suffering or unhappiness. Constant awareness of the reality leads to wisdom and gives you freedom from all misery and bondage. Once you have known the ultimate truth, you will be enlightened and your purpose of life will be fulfilled.

You can postpone everything else, but don't postpone enlightenment. You're not making effort to be happy or to enlighten yourself here and now because you are expecting to be happy in the next world. Don't wait to be enlightened in the next world, because that is not going to happen. Don't think that when you become old you will go to a monastery where you will meet a sage who will bless you and you will automatically be enlightened. Or that when you go to sleep, an angel will come down and take your soul to heaven, where he will polish it and then return it to you. These ideas stem from laziness. Don't postpone happiness and freedom for the unknown life or for the next life. You don't have to wait for death to attain moksha. You can be liberated here and now if you go to the deeper levels of your being. The instant you become aware of the mighty ocean of bliss, you will be cut off from the individual vehicle of the unconscious and you will no longer be an individual; you will become cosmic. It is your choice. When your consciousness travels to the higher dimensions, and finally to the center of consciousness, you will be free from the individual boundaries that make you suffer. The greatest suffering exists because of your separation from the reality. When you are free from body consciousness and individuality, you will be one with the reality and you will no longer experience any suffering. Deep down in the silence of the inner chamber of your being there is someone seated that does not move yet makes your being move. He does not move because He is everywhere. You don't need anyone else. You have Atman within you, the real source of life.

There was one sage who was about to leave his body. When his disciples started to chant God's name, he said, "Hey, stop. What are you doing?"

One person said, "Sir, we are chanting God's name because you taught us to do this."

The sage said, "Stop this chanting and don't disturb me. Of which God are you talking?"

"Sir, you taught us there is only one God."

He said, "What do you mean by one God?"

One of the disciples answered, "Oh, that great Rama, or Krishna or Buddha."

The sage said, "No. Sit down."

He asked another person, "Why are you repeating this god's name?"

He said, "He is the One who has created the universe."

"You also sit down."

Another person said, "Sir, we are referring to that mighty god who lives above the clouds."

The sage told him to leave and asked someone else the same question.

He replied, "He is the one who has built all the great religions and churches and temples."

The sage told him to get out and not to come back again. Finally, he asked someone else, "Whose name are you chanting?"

At last he received the answer he was looking
for: "The God who is in me and in you, Sir."

The sage said, "Yes, you can chant now."

When you pray you should understand to which god
you are praying. Learn to pray to be in communion with
the One who is directly within you and who is the very
essence of life. All the scriptures say God is omnipresent,
omniscient and omnipotent. But theoretical knowledge
is not going to enlighten you. As long as you believe in
theory and do not practise, you will continue to suffer.
Patanjali says the source of your suffering is that you are
not aware of your inner potentials or how to apply them.
He is talking about knowledge of all the modifications,
the whole lake of life within.

When you do tapas, it is action. Any action you
perform will give some result, but there is no such action or
ceremony that can give you emancipation. In this way not
only is action different from knowledge it is also inferior
to knowledge. Knowledge from the very beginning has its
cause and effect in knowledge.

Human beings are the highest of all living beings.
As a human being you have the capacity to understand
yourself and the mystery of how the universe has been
manifested. But you have to stop trying to measure the
whole world with the small mind and realize there are
other ways of knowing. Let your knowing progress to
understanding and your understanding evolve to Self-
realization.

The height of enlightenment is the realization that God is within. If you ask a child in the West where is God, the child will point upward to the sky; a child in the East will point to his chest. Both are right. God is both here and there. The knowledge of the reality has no particular ideology and does not belong to any particular group or *dharma* (law). The Self of all is one and the same. Knowledge is knowledge, light is light and darkness is absence of light.

The life stream is flowing from eternity to eternity, but you are creating barriers and not allowing it to flow without impedance. It is your interference that is bringing you misery and pain. Knowledge requires spontaneity. If you allow that which is flowing to come forward and do not create any barriers to it, you will know whatever you want to know. My master used to say: "You are already God, so there is no need to try to know God. That divine part is already there within you. All you have to do is be a good human being so that the reality can flow spontaneously through you."

The best of knowledge comes through revelation, not through the mind. It is a flood of knowledge that overwhelms the whole being.

Asmita Is the Failure to Comprehend the True Nature of the Soul

The greatest obstacle after avidya is *asmita* (egotism, or self-centeredness). *Asmi,* the first part of the word *asmita,* means "I am;" *-ta* means "-ness." To become egotistical means to go to the darkness of ignorance. Asmita is the failure to comprehend the true nature of the soul.

Ego is the strongest aspect of your *chitta* (the storehouse of your memory; the unconscious mind). Ego separates and limits itself, and creates barriers between you and the reality. Because of ego, you constantly identify with what you are not and at the same time you are not aware of what you are. Ego helps you to expand your consciousness in the external world but not in the internal world. You may be able to recognize and analyze many things but you do not understand yourself. You often say, "I'm fully conscious of such and such," but consciousness related to an external object is not consciousness of a higher order.

Ego has two sides: lower ego and higher ego. Lower ego is the aspect of ego that limits you and builds boundaries that separate you from the whole. Though the lower ego may give you some flashes of knowledge within those boundaries, it does not help you to go beyond. Instead, it drags you down to body consciousness and the objects of the world. The lower ego always wants confirmation and attention and it creates a lot of problems for you.

If you do not train ego, it can be very harmful to you, no matter how knowledgeable or powerful you may be. You can use your ego to perform your worldly duties and to help you become successful in the external world, but don't allow it to be so predominant that you constantly focus on I. Ego should not create barriers for you in the process of your spiritual development. If you purify ego, you can do tremendous things. But if you continue to encourage ego, one day you will find that you have become perfectly egotistical. When someone praises you, you think you are wonderful and can do anything you want to do. However if someone says something negative about you, you feel hurt and become emotional. Either way you are feeding your ego. The way to deal with this is to not accept any praise personally. Surrender it to the Lord because all that is good and great belongs to Him. Remember that you are being praised because of the reality within you, the one and only life force. If you feed your ego with self-centeredness, you will become more egocentric; if you feed it with higher thoughts and use it for something creative, it will become an instrument to help you become aware of the reality. The higher ego can be a great teacher.

If you purify the lower ego, you will become aware of the fact that all living beings are inhaling the same vital force, and therefore there is no reason to be afraid of anyone. As long as you dwell on the plane of duality where you think others are different from you, naturally you will be afraid. Though it is true that physically you look different from others, and your language, culture and thought patterns are different, beneath all these differences lies something that is not different: the absolute truth within everyone is one and the same.

Actually there is no god who separated one soul from another. The term *jiva* (individual soul) is just a superimposition. We are all waves in the vast ocean of bliss. This will be easier to understand by the following analogy: There is a glass inside a room. The space inside the glass, the space inside the room, and the space outside are one and the same. The boundaries of the glass and the room are merely superimpositions on that space. Space is space, and Atman is Atman. The jiva is an individual soul because of its attachment with a particular vehicle or set of instruments that includes mind and its modifications. The one who is driving that vehicle is attached to it. As long as someone uses a vehicle, whether human or animal, that someone is called jiva. You are individual because of the vehicle of the unconscious mind. If you drop that vehicle, you and the reality will be one and the same. All the different forms in the universe have come from the absolute truth, which is beyond name and form. The moment the individual soul returns to its origin, it is no longer individual. It is free.

It is only because you remain attached to the vehicle of the unconscious that you appear to be separate, like a drop of water. The day you meet the ocean, you become the ocean. Qualitatively you and the ocean are the same, but not quantitatively. By thinking that you are an individual, you remain isolated from the whole. When you talk to somebody you don't realize you are talking to yourself. That is why you are suffering and have fears, anxieties and pains. Fear is a great obstacle on the path of enlightenment. When you realize there is one underlying principle, you will be free from all fears. To gain this freedom you will have to expand your individuality to cosmic consciousness. The key point lies in awareness. Today you may be aware of your home, environment, family, nation and all of humanity. The day you become aware of that center from where consciousness flows on different grades and degrees, you will be in touch with the cosmic consciousness and you will be free. If you are fearful, it means you do not realize there is one Absolute here, there and everywhere.

When ego is not aware of another existence that is higher than ego, it keeps growing stronger. But there is a way to help this ego. It is not necessary to break it into pieces or crush it. If you make the small ego aware that there is something bigger behind it, the ego problem will end. As long as you are not aware of the reality, you will continue to think you are everything. Your duty is to establish the supreme *I* in place of the little *I*.

All individuals have all the qualities of the one Universal Self, or God. We are all children of God. All the blood that is flowing in your veins has come from God. If you put billions of persons in a row, you would see that architect has never repeated a face. What a great miracle it is that everyone's face is unique, and still His resources are not exhausted. Who else could be responsible for such a miracle?

Asmi means "I am." Only God, the one reality, can say, "I am One," but two cannot because two are not one. Two has no existence of its own because two exists only on the existence of one. Only one can declare, "I exist." As a human being you cannot say, "I exist," because tomorrow you may not exist like this. When ego says, "I exist," this is false identification. Instead of saying *I*, you should say, "*You* exist," and then *I* won't have ego.

"I am thine, and thou art mine. You exist and I exist, but I exist because of you. I acknowledge my existence, but realize it is because of you." Ego should not be enveloped with pride but with surrender, so that ego shines, until finally you acknowledge, "This is all your grace."

All Things Belong to the **LORD**

Next comes *raga*. Raga means "attachment toward the objects of the world due to the misconception of their true nature." In order to understand raga, let us first examine the principles of pain and pleasure.

Pain and pleasure come from the same source and are limited to individual experience. When mind is not in touch with matter it records no sensation; when mind relates with matter through the senses, it experiences pain and pleasure. Regarding your relationship with the world, it is essential to realize it is not the objects of the world that create problems for you, but the values you put on them. If you like something, it naturally follows that you become attached to it. As long as what you dearly love is with you, it remains a source of pleasure. That same object of pleasure inevitably becomes a potential source of constant disturbance to you because you are afraid you might lose it. And if the person or thing that you love is actually lost, you feel even more pain. For example, if suddenly the news comes that a stranger's son has died, you don't weep. But if you find out that your son has died, then you feel pain. You suffer on account of the fear that comes from self-created attachment to the things of the world.

You have many such unconscious fears that continue to build up within your mind and heart because you have never examined them. When you are enjoying something, never forget that all pleasures reside in the storehouse of pain. It is best not to become attached to anything in the external world, for you will only be disappointed. This is a lesson my master taught me early in my life:

In my youth I lived for some time with my master in a small thatched hut beneath a tree at a place called Jhari at Rishikesh. One day a very rich man came with twelve other people, all carrying baskets of fruits and bundles of money. As I was sitting outside the hut the man came to me and said, "Brahmachari, I want to see your master."

"I will consider it. What else do you want?" I asked.

"I have brought baskets of fruits," the man answered.

I told him we could not possibly eat so much fruit. My master used to say, "If you keep many fruits for tomorrow, at night the wild boars will come and disturb us."

He had also taught me not to eat too much, and that little was enough.

I said, "I will take one or two fruits and that is all. I don't want to attract wild animals to come and eat them."

He looked at me with disappointment and asked, "But surely you will take the money?"

I had instructions from my master to never accept money from anybody. I used to always get what I wanted, so there was no need to do so. When I did not respond, the rich man asked his servants to hand over the bundles of money to me. I looked at all of it and remembered my master telling me that when you need food, you need food, not a collection of paper money. I asked the man, "Where is the money? This is just paper, not money. What good is this paper?"

Before he could reply, my master called from inside the hut, "Who is there? Is somebody troubling you? Let him come."

Relieved to finally be free of me, the rich man hurried inside, bowed before my master and announced proudly, "Sir, I would like to give you one *lakh* (one hundred thousand) rupees."

At that time, one lakh was considered to be a lot of money. My master told me to spread the notes out on the floor. So I opened the bundles and did so. Then he told me to sit, so I sat down on them.

"Do you feel comfortable?" he asked.

I shook my head decisively from side to side.

"Now, sit on the cushion and tell me which is more comfortable."

I replied, "The cushion is much more comfortable."

To sit in meditation you need a cushion, not money. You can have the best of comforts, but don't get attached to them. Never forget this formula: *All the things of the world are meant for me to use, but they do not belong to me.* Accept all the things that you have and enjoy them as God's grace, but don't try to possess them, for they are not yours.

You have come to this world for a short time. The world was here before you came and will remain after you go. This is just a station, a camp in the eternal journey, so it is important not to be caught by the things of the world. Your life is in motion. If you understand the practical principles in life, you can move skillfully and enjoy every step and action. On this journey you will meet many people and create countless relationships. Some will be your friends, colleagues or relatives; others may hate you. All that is irrelevant. The important thing is not to expect too much from the things of the world or from your relationships. You expect something that is not there, and it is your attachment and expectations that make you miserable. You think you can own the things of the world and try to claim them as yours. Nature will take them away from you the moment you think you possess them, and you will become unhappy. Actually a human being has nothing in the world. Nature has given this world to you to enjoy, but your idea of enjoying something is to possess it. As a result, instead of enjoying it, you become attached to it, and misery predictably follows. Attachment is an obstacle that creates bondage and its concomitants, misery and pain. You have the right to enjoy the things of the world, but you should not try to own them because they are not yours and can be snatched away at any time. If you develop that understanding with all the things of the world and with all relationships, you will experience much less sorrow in life.

One way to enjoy life in the world is to adopt an attitude of renunciation. This does not mean you should retreat from the world and your duties and responsibilities; it simply means to renounce attachment. Those who renounce the world cripple themselves and are not able to adjust with others, while those who claim to be happy in the world do not know how to remain unaffected by worldly fetters. Because of temptations and sense gratification, you become attached to the things of the world. Nonattachment does not mean you should not have things. You can have anything you want but don't be attached to it. The attachments that bind you are mainly three: marriage partner, children and property. Only someone who truly renounces these three is free and can be called a renunciate. A renunciate does not renounce breathing or doing ablutions; he renounces those karmas that bind him and create attachment for him. Human beings are miserable because they have forgotten that all the things they have are gifts from the Lord. If you remember that all things belong to the Lord and offer everything to the Lord, you can truly enjoy the world.

Your essential nature is truth. You should have only one desire, to see the face of truth. Identify with the face of truth, not with the glittering rays of the world that completely dissipate your energy. The more scattered your mind is, the more desires you have to fulfill, the more attachments you create and the more you land into a whirlpool of desires that will never allow you to be at peace. Desire breeds desire. Even if you have only a few prominent desires, those desires will keep on breeding until there is no end to it. Desires add fuel to the fire of misery and entanglement and create disaster in life. Desire is the motivation behind your thoughts and emotions and that is why you function in the external world. Your emotions are directed by your desires, not by your mind. Emotion means desire. You are constantly being swayed by your emotions. Sometimes you become very depressed and passive, while at other times you are very active and positive. You do not have a single emotion that is not related to others. You could never be emotional if you didn't have relationships in the world. Life is relationship. But life is divided into two parts: life within and life without. Externally you are related to your close family members, your neighbors, your coworkers and your country. Internally your body is related to your breath, and your body and breath are related to your senses, mind and the center of consciousness. When you have understood all these relationships, you will be able to better organize your emotions. However there will always be a conflict between life within and life without. This is why you should have desires that help you and don't create more obstacles for you. The desire for the higher world should be the dominant desire in your life.

Those who truly renounce, renounce their desires. If you renounce your wife, children and home, it has no meaning if you do not also renounce your desires, lust and attachments. This requires tremendous inner strength. You desire to enjoy the things of the world because you haven't realized there is something much greater beyond that enjoyment. If you trust in the Lord within, you will have inner strength. For that you have to go to the innermost place where the source of light and consciousness dwells. When you become aware of that center, you will be able to withdraw shakti from there.

You argue it is not possible for you not to be attached to your marriage partner and your family. I am not telling you not to love your spouse; I am telling you not to be attached. There is a vast difference between attachment and love. That which brings misery is attachment, not love. You repeat the word love a thousand times throughout the day without actually understanding what it is. You may say you love your boyfriend because you are attached to him. That is not really love. Love has a sense of equality; attachment does not. Love is life and knowledge; attachment has no life. In love you give selflessly and do not expect anything in return; in attachment you want to take and possess things and you have no concept of what it means to give. When you possess something, you are just expanding the domain of your ego; when you love and you are a giver, you are surrendering your ego.

Attachment is always a source of misery, no matter who or what you are attached to, while love is a source of liberation. Attachment is dependent on others or on a particular object that will inevitably change, whereas love is dependent purely on knowledge and the reality. For example, if the person whom you claim to love changes, your feelings for that person will also change. Being attached to someone may give you pleasure, but that attachment could also lead you to *dvesha.*

Dvesha means "repulsion or feelings of hatred for persons or things." Raga and dvesha, attachment and hatred, are two sides of the same coin. You cannot separate them. Dvesha may cause pain when one is confronted with an object or a person one does not like or when such an aversion assumes the form of contempt, hatred or open hostility. When you become attached you become blind and forget the reality. When you are attached to certain things, they create such strong impressions in your mind that you remember those things again and again. The impressions that hatred creates are even deeper. When you hate somebody you forget all about those whom you love, because hatred is stronger than love. If you really want to understand the capacity of your love, just watch how strong your hatred is for certain persons or things. If you love somebody wholeheartedly, you can never hate that person.

Patanjali says constant contemplation over the opposite is the way to get freedom from hatred and violence. Thought power is very important. Even though you have the capacity to do so, you have not learned how to direct negative emotions toward positive grooves. If somebody hates you, try to think of that person in a loving way. Don't torture yourself by thinking about somebody negatively. It is very harmful to think or meditate negatively. When you hate others, it is you who suffers. Learn to forgive. The same life force is within you and everyone else. Learn to love and live with that life force and give the best that you have selflessly. Live in the world and love all, excluding none. If you are a giving person and love selflessly, nobody can snatch your happiness from you. Love is the source of liberation and has the power to transform you. Love is life.

Make the best use of all the things of the world that you have, but never be attached to them. When you become attached you are in bondage. Even though you create this misery for yourself, still you pray to God to give you freedom. God replies, "I have given you will, power, brilliance and intelligence. Why do you not do it yourself?" If you want to be free from physical pain you can go under anesthesia, but at the same time you will be unconscious. It would be better to make effort to expand your consciousness. Because mind is more powerful than body, if you learn to control your mind you can easily eliminate physical pain. However, although anesthesia can give you freedom from physical pain, there is no such anesthesia that can give freedom from pain on deeper levels. You cannot philosophically deny that such pain exists. You all know that when you have to face the reality of losing someone who is very dear and close to you, how painful it is. Nobody can share or understand the pain that you are feeling at that time. You have to go to the root of the pain and try to understand the cause of pain, not its effect. Nothing can help you if you do not look within and free yourself from the bondage you have created for yourself.

The goal of life is to attain everlasting joy and happiness. For that you will have to turn within. Because your mind remains dissipated, you have not assimilated this truth. Attachment to the objects of the world consumes all your time and energy so you don't have the time or awareness to attain your goal. You identify with the objects of the world and remain lost in the world, having forgotten your true Self. It is human nature to want pleasures to last forever, so you keep searching in the external world for something that will give you unlimited peace and happiness. External objects can give you momentary joys, but those joys can never be perfectly satisfying. After every joy you experience, you feel some grief or sorrow because you are not able to retain that joy for a long time. Even though you know worldly joy is not complete, at the same time you want it to be everlasting. The things in the external world do not have the capacity to give everlasting joy. Everlasting happiness is within. You may think the objects of the world are giving you joy, but in reality all your joys are coming from within. The senses, mind and ego cannot reach there because it is beyond all of these. You are like the musk deer in the mountains that carries a fragrance within itself. It smells that fragrance and runs wildly here and there all over the forest in search of it because it doesn't know the fragrance is coming from itself. Likewise you are restlessly running around in search of peace, unaware that peace lies within. You complain you have sincerely been working hard, yet you have not been successful. Along with sincerity, action and devotion you need knowledge.

With all the material prosperity and wisdom of the eternal world that humanity has been able to attain, still you find only darkness within. I have not met a single human being who is truly happy. The external world offers many means and comforts but if you have no goal, you allow these means to distract you instead of applying them to attain a goal. Anyone who knows something about life is searching for something, but doesn't know what it is. You go to a temple, a church or a teacher, you study books, you do different types of work, but still you do not seem to be in a state of equilibrium. It means there is a spiritual crisis in your daily life. I am not saying that life in the external world is not important. You have to face the external world. You cannot isolate yourself from the world and sit under a tree or in a quiet and calm place and expect to be happy. You have to deal with the external world and your relationships in the external world. You have to continue to do your duties and function in the external world. The external world can help you to attain the goal of life only if you do not allow it to create problems for you.

Peace is not a gift that God gives to you or to anyone else. That is not His work. Likewise God did not create nuclear weapons or any of the external amenities that you have. But God has given you the capacity and all the talents that you need. Yet you cripple yourself by postponing everything in the name of God. It is good to believe in God, but it is not good to refrain from doing your actions. No one else, not even a guru or a swami, no matter how great, can give you peace. The way to attain peace is by not being attached to the things of the world and by decreasing useless desires. A Sufi sage has endorsed this message of non-attachment:

There was once a Sufi sage in the Punjab region of India. All the intellectuals of the city went to him for advice and they asked, "Sir, please tell us one thing to practice in order to see God. Please give us that one truth."

He replied, "It is very easy to meet God. Presently you are connected to the external world. Just disconnect yourself here and connect yourself there. Actually you are already there."

If you are not attached to anything and you are doing your duties skillfully, you will have peace. This requires human effort. Only those who are established in Atman, free from attachments and desires, are fully at peace. Learn to love, to grow in love and to be in love. Love is pure and divine.

DEATH Means SEPARATION,
Not Complete Annihilation

Abhinivesha is the inordinate, abject fear of death. Your greatest fear is that you will die. Even though you know that no one has ever lived on earth forever, you remain under the pressure of the fear of death and pain. Your mind remains more occupied with the fear of death than with death itself because you don't understand what it is. You hesitate to even talk about death because it is too terrifying to you. Not only do you worry about what will happen to your wealth and all the objects and people you love if you should die, you wonder what will happen to you after death and where you will go. You can only imagine what type of world the subtle world is and you worry about going to hell. You can rest assured there is no such authority that sends you to heaven or hell. These are just mental concepts meant to create fear in your mind and heart, and you should resolve such fears here and now. That which is going to happen is going to happen, and that which is not going to happen will never happen. In either case, why worry? No matter how much you cry or worry about it, you are sure to die. Death is an inevitable natural phenomenon everyone has to accept. I learned from experience that it is better to be more curious about it than afraid:

Once I was forced to face the fear of death. My master had advised me to have a retreat every year. During this retreat I was to remain in complete solitude for nine days in a place where I would meet nobody. The purpose for such a retreat is to become aware of and to confront what is hidden within the unconscious. One October I was asked to go as usual for such a retreat. While I was on this retreat I was walking along the side of a mountain, and my wooden sandals slipped on some pine needles, causing me to fall. I rolled down the mountain a distance of about 500 yards, until a thorny bush interrupted my fall. Actually the reason I stopped falling was that a branch of that bush had pierced my abdomen, and I remained hanging from that branch. When I looked down, I could see a stream of blood running down the rock. To make matters worse, the branch I was stuck on kept swaying forward and backward. My weight caused the branch to swing forward, and the pull of the bush would bring me back. I could see the fast current of the river below and knew if I fell into the water, there would be no chance of swimming. It seemed there was no way out and I was sure I was going to die very soon. In my fear I kept remembering all the mantras to which I had been exposed. I thought if none of the Hindu mantras worked, I would try Buddhist, Tibetan and Christian mantras. I even knew some Jewish mantras. Even though I tried all the different mantras, nothing helped. Because of the loss of blood, I was beginning to lose consciousness, but my fear of death was so intense, I was hardly aware of any pain. I could see the stream of blood and I could feel some pain, but the predominant thoughts revolved around my fear of death. I didn't want to die without having accomplished anything because I knew I would have to come back and work hard again from childhood. I was not worried about being born again, but about having to be completely dependent on others initially. I knew that nature does not accommodate you and make you a wise man immediately just because you were a swami in your previous life. You have to repeat the whole process. These thoughts kept going through my mind because I thought death was certain. I kept praying to all the great sages and gods, but nothing happened. I remained suspended from that bush for at least a half hour. Finally some women who had come to cut the elephant grass that was growing there noticed me. One of them said, "Oh, he must be dead."

I thought, *My, Lord, if they leave me like this thinking I'm dead, I surely will die.*

Since my head was hanging down, I started to move my feet and legs. One of them saw the movement and said, "Look, he's moving. Let's try to save him."

Fortunately they had a long rope with them. They came to me and tied the rope around me. Up to that moment I had hardly felt any physical pain. But since I no longer felt the fear of death, I became very aware of the pain, and it was so severe I almost lost consciousness. I caught myself as I thought, *They are not doctors. It's probably not a good idea to lose consciousness.*

The women helped me down to the road. Soon thereafter my master appeared and said, "It's nothing. Don't worry. You have suffered, but you'll be okay now."

Since there were no hospitals or medicines in the mountains, my master collected some herbs, crushed them and applied them to the wound. Then he took me back to the cave where I had been staying and said, "You still have to complete your nine-day retreat."

I knew those nine days would be more difficult because of the pain.

Many people think death is the greatest of all tragedies, but to a fortunate few the idea of dying is a matter of fact, like the end of a school year. Life is a series of changes and death is one of those changes. Nothing happens to you when you die because your subtle existence is not subject to change; only your form changes. Death is nothing but a habit of the body. The body is matter, and it is the dharma of all matter to change, die and go to decomposition.

In order to understand death it is essential to look beyond the physical body to the other levels that make up the complex human organism. You see yourself only at the superficial level of the body and have accepted without question that you are limited to the body. When you say *I,* you are referring to your physical body. Your body is everything to you and you look after it as though it were your greatest friend. You don't realize this friend of yours is very weak. If you continue to identify solely with the body, you will also become very weak. When you study yourself and come to know yourself from within you will find you are something entirely different than what you thought you were.

It is not just the body that defines a human being. Yoga gives a more complete definition: *a human being is an individual soul, jiva, having a life force with certain vehicles or instruments.* You have an individual unconscious mind and a conscious mind, and you are a breathing being with a physical body. Beyond the body is the mind, and the soul is even deeper than the mind. It is not the mind or the body that experiences the waking state and the gross world of external objects. There is only one who experiences and that is the individual soul or jiva, also called atman. The individual atman is to be distinguished from the Atman that is the pure light of knowledge or truth that dwells in the space within every human being's subtle heart and pervades the entire being. This Atman manifests *prana* (the life force), mind, senses and body, and this is how you exist. It is a force that comes directly from the center of pure consciousness.

According to yoga there are five sheaths or external coverings of the Atman within you. *Annamaya kosha,* the physical body, is like a garment or external sheath for the subtler levels. Subtler than the physical sheath is the pranic or energy sheath, *pranayama kosha,* and even subtler is *manomaya kosha,* the mental sheath. The subtlest sheaths are *vijnanamaya kosha,* the buddhi, and *anandamaya kosha,* the sheath of bliss.

Physically and on the sense level you may be limited to the body, but on the mental level you are not. And on the highest level of consciousness you are one with the reality. But if you continue to identify with your body throughout your whole life, you will never know Atman consciousness. You are conscious of your body and the changes of your body, but you are not aware that beneath all these changes there is within you something that never changes and is not subject to any movement. You are living under the misconception that the functioning of your body and senses is autonomous because you are ignorant of the inner source of intelligence that motivates you to think, hear, understand, speak and move. Because of the soul everything moves, but the soul itself is not subject to movement because there is no power beyond the soul to create movement in it. Your body moves, your senses move and your mind moves, but the truth within you does not move because it is already everywhere. If you go within to the source you will find your greatest friend waiting to embrace you. You cannot know that source through the mind because it is beyond mind.

With this description of the five sheaths and Atman, it becomes easier to explain the process of death. Actually you are three selves: mortal, semi-immortal and totally immortal. Your perishable or mortal self includes the body, breath, senses and conscious mind. The unconscious mind and the atman make up the unknown and semi-immortal self, which is the individual soul, jiva. The soul is beyond body, breath, senses and mind. It is called semi-immortal because the immortal soul is linked with the vehicle of the unconscious, which gives it individuality. You are individual not only because you think and behave differently, but also because of personal habit patterns, desires and samskaras that are stored in the reservoir of the unconscious mind as memory. The third self is the pure universal Atman, who, without any superimposition, is immortal. Jiva is in the bondage of its own actions, but Atman is not in bondage. Jiva is like a drop of water and Brahman or Atman is the ocean. Qualitatively they are one and the same.

Only the known and mortal part of you — body, senses, breath and conscious mind — is subject to change, death and destruction. As long as you are inhaling and exhaling, your mind and body remain together and work together and you live in the world. The breath is the bridge between the body and the mind. In the process of dying, the breath ceases and the body and senses no longer function. When this takes place, mind withdraws itself from the external world, and the conscious mind fails. Though the conscious mind fails, the unconscious mind and the individual soul continue to exist. At the time of death the unconscious mind and the soul separate from the body and the conscious mind. So death means separation of the mortal self from the semi-immortal self.

Death is only a transition. After dropping the body you cross this mire of delusion and go to the other shore. No matter where you go, your unconscious mind goes with you. The unconscious mind is the vehicle for the individual soul to continue to exist in the subtle world. You drive the vehicle of the unconscious to the unknown world, with all your desires, memories and impressions of your experiences. It is those experiences that motivate you to come back again. At the time of death the unconscious mind will reveal to you what you have stored there. As long as you are using this vehicle, even after death you will remain an individual soul with your unconscious mind, although you will not have a body, senses or breath and you will not be conscious of yourself. The moment you drop that vehicle, you will be free. For example, if you break down the walls of a house, it will no longer be a house. It is only the superimposition of the walls that separates the space within the house from the space outside.

You diligently prepare your external world so you have all the comforts and means you need, but you have never considered preparing yourself to go through the period of transition during the process of dying. The scriptures emphasize the importance of skillful and selfless actions so you will not have to be afraid of the unconscious mind at the end. If you have prepared yourself, during the process of departing you will be able to remember all the good things you have done instead of dwelling on sad memories and past experiences that create depression or fear in the mind. That is why it is very important to do sadhana.

With the above clarification of the process of dying you can better understand the concepts of heaven and hell. You don't go to heaven or hell or anywhere else after death. God never makes anyone miserable or happy and never sends anyone to heaven or hell. You create misery or happiness by your thoughts, emotions and desires, and by not organizing your internal and external life. In this way you create heaven or hell for yourself here on earth. Wherever you are can become hell if you don't make effort to improve yourself. This modern world is creating hell for modern people, and God is not responsible for that. Anybody who is materialistic will definitely die with those impressions stored in the unconscious mind when he casts off the body. So naturally that person will remain in a state of ignorance that is definitely more terrifying than hell. According to me, hell is a state of ignorance that a human being creates by being too materialistic and too occupied with sensual pleasures, and by identifying with the objects of the world instead of making effort to realize his true nature, which is peace, happiness and bliss. Life gives to you only what you have within; it doesn't give you something you don't already have. If you select only the negative part, you will suffer. Negative thinking leads you to a hellish way of life. In addition, the more negative you are, you more you cripple your willpower. Don't allow that to happen. Always remember you have some good within also. Positive thinking and selflessness can lead you to happiness and a state of freedom from pain and misery.

The kingdom of God is within, so there is no need to aspire to go to heaven after death. If you make sincere effort, you can create heaven through your mind, actions and speech. You can establish heaven here and now if you understand the various aspects of your chitta and you discipline yourself. You are fully equipped to do that. You keep talking about how you are going to enjoy tomorrow. This means you associate enjoyment with the future instead of here and now. It is not possible that you could be happy after death but not here and now. If you can learn to enjoy here and now, you will become aware of eternity.

You live in the physical realm in your habit patterns, and you will remain entangled in the snare of those same habit patterns after death. So if you understand your habit patterns, you know where you are going after death. Death has no power to change you or release you from your habit patterns. Don't waste your time waiting for heaven after death or thinking death will relieve you from all pain and misery. This misconception that death will provide freedom from suffering is unfortunately the reason people tragically opt for suicide as a way out. The fact is you will go to the next life in the same state as you are here. If you are ignorant here, death can never give you solace or liberate you from that ignorance. It is just like waking up to another day and finding that you are the same as you were yesterday. If you are a fool today, you will not wake up wise tomorrow. Just as sleep does not solve your financial problems, and you have to face them the next day, death doesn't change anything. It only makes you forget for a while. Your next birth will bring forward what you have forgotten. Don't think that by being in a deep state of sleep you will be relieved of something, or that by being born again you will receive something better. Death cannot change your circumstances. If you are disappointed and frustrated with life, don't expect death to relieve you from that pain. That is not going to happen. You will have to transform yourself here in this life by becoming aware. When you are inside a room, you are aware of the walls of that room. If you want to be aware of something more, you will have to go out of that room. Only through sadhana and working with yourself on all levels — physical, mental and spiritual — can you change your habit patterns and transform your personality.

The first step is to decide you want to be healthy and that you are going to be healthy; then take charge of your health by eliminating injurious dietary and sedentary habits. If the body is creating problems for you, remember mind is more powerful than body. The breath is the link between mind and body. By including breathing and relaxation practices in your daily sadhana you can directly affect both your physical and mental health. You can transform negative thinking habits and even deep samskaras through the regular practice of meditation and by constant awareness that the reality is within you. Then there will be no need to feel sad or to condemn yourself. This is the holistic approach to self-training in which you work with yourself on all levels. Without working hard you cannot accomplish anything. If you remain afraid to encounter the fears you have created for yourself on the superficial level, you will never get the opportunity to see the finest and most glorious part of yourself, your inner Self. You will have to face yourself sooner or later, because at the time of death all communication with others will come to a halt, and you will be all alone. Then you will have to depend on your inner strength. You went through birth alone and you will have to go through the lonely passage of death. Sadhana will help you to be very strong from within so this transition does not affect you negatively. Death has no power to change you, but you have tremendous power to transform yourself by changing your level of awareness. Otherwise the physical field of awareness will continue to bind you and you will remain roaming in this field only, which is probably not such a great thing:

Once there was a man who persistently prayed to the Lord to let him become immortal. The Lord said, "My son, you have served me well and you have been praying with a single-pointed mind. Tell me what it is that you want."

"I want my body to be immortal," he answered.

"You want your body to be immortal even though the nature of the body is subject to

change, death, decay and decomposition? Why
do you have such a desire?" God asked.

He said, " I have only this one desire. If you are
the Lord of life and of the universe, please give
me this boon."

God replied, "I will make you immortal, but
before my boon comes into effect and your
desire is fulfilled, go to that mountain and
drink the water of the fountain there."

The man rushed to the fountain and was
surprised to see many persons crying there.
One of them saw him and warned him, "Stop.
Don't drink this water. Don't you see we are all
suffering here? Do you also want to suffer? It is
useless to wish for a long span of life without
any purpose. If you want a long life just so you
can continue to enjoy the objects of the senses,
don't do this or you will suffer. If you were
to become physically eternal, you could not
tolerate the burden of worries. The long sleep
called death is a great relief. Don't try to avoid
this sleep."

Finally he realized that there is something
beyond the senses and the mind. He understood
that only the kingdom of Atman within could
liberate him.

You desire to live for a long time because you are not
aware that there is only one unifying principle, Brahman.
Brahman and Atman are one and the same. And who are
you? Thou art That. You are a living shrine in which the

Lord of life is dwelling. The day you attain this awareness, you will go beyond the concepts of past, present and future. You have come to fulfill a certain purpose and that purpose is to become aware of the One Absolute beneath all forms and names. With this awareness will come freedom from all fears. As long as you believe you are only a drop of water, you will remain afraid that you will be lost somewhere or absorbed by the earth. When you become the ocean you will no longer be afraid. Your body is a good instrument, but don't identify yourself with the body so much that you lose awareness of the Lord within. You are suffering because you have forgotten that you are Atman. The moment you become aware of it, you will be free. To develop this awareness you will have to do sadhana.

In this cycle that is rotating from eternity to eternity, it is not easy to get a human body. Don't waste this opportunity that Providence has given you by living only on the sense level. Enjoy life but don't be lost in superficial enjoyments or create attachments to the material world. No object in the external world, no matter how great it is, can ever help you to realize the truth. It is your strong attachment to life that does not allow you to be free:

There was one old woman who was very wealthy and owned several buildings. Neither her grandsons nor her own sons cared for her and they did not visit her. She had everything except human love. So she prayed and prayed for death to come and take her. Prayer means a strong desire and all desires, provided you know how to apply the means to achieve the object of your desires, are fulfilled sooner or later.

And so one day, death came in a black robe to fulfill her wish. "Who are you?" she inquired.

"You prayed for me to come, so I have come. I am death. Why are you hesitating now? Come with me."

She said, "Look, you can take my suitcase and bedding, but I am not prepared to come now."

You do not know that beneath this superficial world there is something immortal that is not subject to change, death and decay. You are essentially immortal. When you drop all superimpositions, you become perfectly immortal. The totally immortal self is no longer individual. The immortal self is the soul in its purity, or Atman. Know that and be happy. You cannot separate yourself from the reality and immortality. Constant awareness of the reality is the aim of life. With this awareness you can live here and now with happiness in every breath.

Death is like a deep sleep without consciousness. Even in your sleep you do some actions unconsciously. For example, if I were to ask you how many times you turned over in bed during your sleep last night, you couldn't tell me because you were not conscious of those movements. You sleep for eight hours every night; if you sleep for one hundred years, it is called death. As sleep relieves you from many tensions, death temporarily relieves you from the burden of life. To die is not a bad thing, but you are afraid of it. Death is not terrible and fearful; it is the idea of death that is very fearful. Get rid of that idea; live and enjoy life. In order for a seed to germinate and grow it has to break. Once the seed breaks, it is permanently broken. That breaking is like death. Likewise, in order for a flower to blossom, the bud has to break; subsequently, a flower has to break for its fruit to emerge. And when a fruit breaks, many more seeds are released. So actually there is no death for the seed; a seed bears more seeds and the life cycle continues.

Death comes to everyone: the weak and the powerful, the rich and the poor, the fearless and the fearful. Death is bound to happen because it is an essential part of life. You were born, you became a child, then you matured into adulthood, and finally you will become old and death will follow. Today if I were to ask you to show me yourself as a child, it wouldn't be possible for you to become the same child you were years ago because you have grown out of your childhood. All these changes occur in one and the same stream of life. Death is simply the culmination of growth. Any living thing that has completed its growth cycle will die.

Fear of death comes from the fear of leaving what you have and not getting what you want. Death itself is never painful. Pain comes only when you are attached to the things of the world. There is no need to cry or remain under fear. Those who know what death is are not afraid of it. Those who are not conscious of the eternal stream of life remain under the fear of death and cannot enjoy life. They do not know how to live life here and now. The most difficult aspect of death is the period of transition. This is why you should make your mind very strong before casting off the body and try to resolve all the conflicts you have created, so there will be no problem in the end.

Death means change and separation, not complete annihilation. I am qualified to tell you about the death experience because I have gone there and have come back. In our tradition one of the first things we learn is to consciously cast off the body and then to come back. In this way we have direct experience of what occurs during death, and so death is no longer something mysterious or unknown to us, and we are not afraid of it. Actually the word *death* is not used in the monastery. Instead we refer to death as the process of dropping the body. When the body is no longer helpful, it should be dropped. The body is like a garment, and death is nothing but a change of garments. As you change your coat, you can consciously change this garment. It is not difficult. When a yogi feels that the body has become old and is creating obstacles for the mind, he fixes up a time and drops it. This is nothing unusual. Any person who meditates can do it. Of course, God's grace is there, but you also need human effort. You have to make your *sankalpa shakti* (determination) very strong to do this yoga practice.

There are various methods of dropping the body, one of which utilizes the technique of *murcha pranayama*. It actually is a simple thing to drop the body, but control of the breath is absolutely essential. There are two breaths, right and left. The right breath is fire or the sun, and the left is the moon. If you concentrate on the flow of the breath and do not allow the breath to flow through the left nostril, your breath will become active on the right. In the process of dropping the body, yogis block the left breath and start the flow of the right breath. That is the path of fire. By applying the right breath they initiate a silent dialogue with the fire of life.

Expansion of the pause that occurs in the process of breathing is called death. If you learn to eliminate the pause, you can have control over your own death. Death has no power to snatch the body of a real yogi because the death of a yogi is under his will. A yogi creates his own destiny because he has the knowledge of death. My master lived more than 150 years. He was able to do this because he knew how to use certain energy fields for that purpose. The day you come to know the part of you that is keeping you alive, you also can acquire control over going to the other world and coming back. There is no death for those who understand the reality:

There were two sages. One was an expert who could predict anyone's date and time of death. Whoever tested his ability found his predictions to be 100% accurate. He was so sure of himself he stated, "You can kill me the moment one of my predictions is wrong."

One day a yogi came to him and he told that yogi, "I see that you are going to die at such and such place on such and such day."

The yogi said, "No, you are wrong. Death means separation of the two vehicles, prana and apana, that are supplying life energy and cleansing the body respectively. I will hide them somewhere where death has no access. We will see about your prediction. I will stay in your home until the predicted time arrives."

Nine times he tried to predict the death of that yogi, and each time the yogi proved him wrong and did not die.

If you know the science of death, your death can be under your control. Death means destruction of the pranic vehicles. If you know how to control the pranic vehicles, you can control death, and no astrology or predictions will ever come true.

If you consciously leave your body, it is not painful. But if death comes, makes you sick, takes you away and leaves your body here, then it is painful. You can learn to consciously and willingly drop your body if you recognize that the body is different from you. You see yourself only as a body, not as the life force. There is no death for the life force that is present from eternity to eternity. That which existed in the past and which exists now, will exist in the future. You cannot change this fact. Know this truth and be free from the ignorance of the multitudes. When you become aware of the difference between that which never dies and that which is subject to death and decay, you will be free. I was able to witness the process of dying consciously several times in the years of my training:

Once I went to see a swami who was at Aligarh. I could not understand how it was possible for a good swami to be at Aligarh because I had the notion that all good swamis were in the Himalayas. I thought it was not possible for a good swami to live on the bank of a small river situated near a city. But I was very keen to learn so I went to see him anyway. When I was still four miles away he sent food to me. I thought, *This is nothing. If someone is coming to see me, I also feel that they are coming and I send food for them. This is not wisdom; it is only common sense.*

When I reached, he said, "You're late. I'm going to leave my body tomorrow morning."

I pleaded, "Couldn't you wait another twelve hours so you could teach me something?"

He refused and said determinedly, "No. I don't have time."

And he walked away.

The Hindus considered him to be a Hindu swami, the Muslims thought he was a Muslim saint, and the Christians were sure he was a great Christian saint. So when he announced that he was going to die, the Hindus insisted they would take him to their burning ghat; the Mohammedans were adamant that his body would remain in their graveyard; and the Christians planned to take him to their cemetery.

The next morning he left his body as he had said he would, and three hours later the doctors came and examined him and declared that he was dead. Then there was great confusion because people from the different communities had come with arms and ammunition and had actually started to fight for the body of that swami. In frustration the district magistrate and the police came to me and said, "You're a swami. Tell us whether he was Hindu or Christian or Mohammedan."

I abruptly replied, "I don't know anything about him."

But they persisted to interrogate me and asked, "If you don't know anything about him, why did you come to see him?"

"In our tradition we don't ask another swami from which house he has come or what his caste is. A swami is a swami."

This made them angry and they put me under police custody. I did not understand why all this was happening and I thought, *What type of swami was he? He died and created problems for me without teaching me anything.*

I spoke to his dead body, "If you were a true swami, you would answer me. I came from the Himalayas to see you, and now the police are telling me I am under arrest. I don't know anything about you. If you were a true swami, you would do something to convince me."

This was four hours after we thought he had left his body. He astounded everyone by suddenly sitting up and complaining, "Look, I am not able to leave because you are all fighting."

The police, the district magistrate and everybody else were shocked and just stared at him. Then he began to shout, "Get out of my sight all of you! You Hindus, Christians and Mohammedans—you are all foolish people. I don't belong to anybody. I belong to God and to no one else. Now I am not going to die. You cannot force me to die."

I asked, "Why did you not tell me yesterday that this was going to happen?"

He hugged me and inquired, "Did they trouble you my son? Don't worry. Now I will stay with you for three days to teach you."

So I stayed and really enjoyed being with him and learning from him. He said to me, "There is nothing higher than the science of breath. Don't waste time going here and there. Learn this science."

And he taught me many techniques. He repeated several times, "Be what you are and don't show off."

On the fourth day he quietly said to me, "Now I really want to go. I have used this body as much as I could. It cannot help me anymore, so I have to leave it. Help me to get into the water."

Later when people came to look for him I showed them the spot in the water where he had taken samadhi (dropped the body). For seven or eight days they searched for his body but could not find it.

There are some great individuals who are born because they want to serve others. They come to the world with the determination to serve humanity, not to enjoy others' hospitality. Such great persons have death under their control and can cast off the body any time they want because they have the knowledge of birth and death. Such a person is called *amara* (immortal). You are more concerned about taking something from the world. That's why you don't know how to consciously drop your body.

The message here is to remain free from the fear of death. Only through knowledge, by understanding what is the mortal part in a human being and what is the immortal part, can you become free from the fear of death. Fear comes from ignorance and attachment. When you are attached to the things of the world, you try to possess them. Then you remain afraid of losing them or of not gaining them again. So attachment is the mother of all fears, and fear always invites danger. But when you become aware of the reality that is not subject to change, death and decay, you will get freedom from that fear. Live here and now by doing your duties to the best of your capacity and enjoy life from moment to moment. Those who fear death are unaware of the reality and do not know how to enjoy. Remember that the Lord is within you because the Lord is omnipresent. Even if you do not believe in the Lord, you should understand there is something called Self-existence, or truth. It is not possible to separate yourself from the truth, and truth has no power to separate itself from you. You are limitless and this universe is an expansion of you.

In each lifetime you are born only once and death comes only once. When you come to this world of phenomena, it is called birth; going back to the latent state is called death. The soul is like a ripple in the ocean. Like a wave it does not go anywhere but remains a part of the ocean. There is no death for the ocean or reality because the reality is omnipresent, omniscient and omnipotent.

We have come from the reality and we live in the reality like waves in the ocean of eternity. Nothing happens to us when we die because the ocean is eternal. If there were no waves, the ocean wouldn't exist. We are the reality.

Abhinivesha means "a strong desire to live; a clinging to life without knowing why; an affliction toward life." This clinging to life makes you miserable and gives you a false sense of self-preservation. You want to live in this world for a long time, but you don't understand what life is or what the purpose of life is. You don't know from where you have come or to where you will go. Life remains a mystery to you because you see everything with two small eyes. You think the small mind has tremendous power to know and analyze everything. Your vision is very limited because you do not know how to see things on different levels or how to apply the different means that you already have. You are here in this world because you have a purpose to fulfill. You think the world is just for enjoyment, remaining oblivious to the fact that the world is actually a means to help you fulfill the purpose of life.

The fear of death comes from ignorance. Lack of knowledge is ignorance, the mother of all fears. You want to enjoy life, and live for a long time but you cannot do it because you remain under the pressure of fears all the time. You are afraid of losing what you have and that you will not gain what you want to gain. Beneath these two is the fear that you might die. This fear stays with you because you are not aware that within you is immortality.

As you progress on the path of spirituality the mysteries of life and death will gradually be revealed to you. You will come to understand that you are a child of immortality and that a part of you never dies. This will help you to develop confidence and you will realize there is no need for worry or fear of death.

In this lifetime you should attain that state of freedom where you can voluntarily dissociate yourself from body consciousness. You cannot make the physical immortal, but you can expand your life span and live for more than one hundred years. You can use the body as an instrument to help you to attain the purpose of life. And when you feel the body is no longer a useful instrument, you have the power to voluntarily withdraw your mind from body consciousness and divert it to the source of consciousness within. No matter how much you cling to life you cannot avoid death, as this story demonstrates:

One day a woman came to Buddha, and said, "O enlightened one! You are all powerful. Please help me. Today, I am very sad."

He said, "Sit down and tell me what the problem is."

"I had only one son, and he died. Only you have the power to bring his life breath back."

"I will definitely do it, provided you do one thing. Go and visit all the homes in our kingdom. If you find any home where nobody has died, come back to me and I will bring this child back to life."

After three days, the woman returned and said, "O Lord, now I am beginning to understand the mystery of life and death."

The mysteries of death and birth are revealed only to wise persons, not to fools. You do not die many times in one lifetime. Everyone has to depart; yet no one believes they will die. This is because there is no death for eternity and you are a child of eternity. Unconsciously you know the best part of you, the soul, will never die. There is no need to aspire to go to heaven after death. You can establish that heaven here and now. If you make sincere effort, heaven is a joy you can create and emanate through your thoughts, speech and actions. First understand the various aspects of your chitta (mind), then do sadhana and discipline yourself.

What appears to be death is but a momentary disappearance, to be revived again in another form. This does not mean your individuality and personality will be lost. Rather your true personality or individuality will extend further and further, until it permeates through all things in the world and is absorbed in the infinite completeness of the whole.

These are the five kleshas that create obstacles on the path: avidya, asmita, raga, dvesha, and abhinivesha. Patanjali says you are here to attain samadhi, to establish yourself in your essential nature. You have not been able to attain samadhi because of the kleshas. You have created the kleshas and you have the power to remove them. Actually, there is nothing like destruction in yoga, but here Patanjali is talking about destruction. To destroy ignorance means to remove it. Since ignorance has no existence of itself, you are not destroying something that exists. It is not possible to destroy anything that has its own existence. You can only destroy what is subject to destruction. Here Patanjali means the removal of all the kleshas will help you on the path to enlightenment.

To get freedom from the kleshas remember the first sutra: *tapas svadhyaya ishvara pranidhana* (control of the senses, self-study and surrender to the Lord within). The three principles of kriya yoga can help you to remove the five kleshas, the obstacles in your path that keep you from attaining samadhi.

Patanjali says it is helpful to understand the five kleshas, but this is not sufficient to obtain freedom. Suppose you have controlled the five kleshas and you are no longer in the darkness of ignorance; you have conquered your egotistical nature, attachment and repulsion, and the affliction of clinging to life. Even then, you would not have conquered everything and so would not immediately attain samadhi. This is because there would still be many modifications of the mind or kleshas deeply rooted with your karmas. You are not aware of these modifications because they are in seed form, hidden in the unconscious. Your unconscious mind keeps a record of everything you do or have ever done, so there is no need to be afraid that someone else is keeping a record of your actions. When you go from this world you carry that record with all the seeds of your karmas with you. Whenever you get the opportunity, you again come forward in a new birth and start doing the same karmas.

It is very difficult to get freedom from the latent kleshas because they are deeply entwined with your karmas. This is why you have to practice preliminary or kriya yoga. Patanjali says that with the help of meditation you can control all the modifications of the kleshas. Later, he explains what type of meditation can help you, but now, before you can deal efficiently with the kleshas, it is important to understand what karma is.

As You SOW, so Shall You REAP

It is easy to understand the Yoga Sutras of Patanjali if you understand the philosophy of the kleshas and the cycle of karma and reincarnation. Karma and reincarnation are twin laws that are inseparable. Patanjali has explained how karma controls our lives and compels us to continue in the cycle of birth and death.

The word *karma* is a Sanskrit word that comes from the root *kri* meaning "to do." Any action that you perform is karma. Some actions are helpful to you and others create obstacles such as anxiety, unhappiness, grief and sorrow.

There are four phases of karma: One phase is to create something, such as making a table out of wood or a pot out of clay. Another phase is modification. For instance, milk can be modified to make butter. The third phase is purification, such as the purification of gold by putting it into fire. And the fourth is movement from one place to another. All actions come under these four phases.

A person cannot live without performing actions. The purpose of karma is to keep you active so that you do not forget and return to a dormant state, a state in which energy is not available for use. For example, even though the atmospheric heat sometimes increases to very high temperatures, you cannot cook your food with that heat. Likewise, if the humidity rises to very high levels, you cannot quench your thirst with that humidity because it is in a dormant state. It is only when that same energy is brought forward in action that it becomes useful. Any action you do in the external world involves movement that you initiate. This action is simply a means to some result. Once you have completed the action, you return to non-action. If there is motion there is also its opposite, stillness or non-motion; if there is action there is non-action. It is like crossing a river. To cross a river you have to know the method of how to cross a river. If you fight against the current you won't go very far; you have to go with the natural motion of the water. When you reach the other shore, you leave the motion of the water.

Although every gesture is an expression of karma, actions cannot be understood by simply analyzing physical gestures because karma is not limited to external actions. Karma includes thoughts, actions, emotions and desires. Any action that you do is preceded by a thought. Your mind does not motivate your limbs to do anything in the external world without thought. However, if a thought pattern comes and vanishes and you do not take any action, it is not karma. Your behavior is different from that of other individuals because you think differently. Without having thought it, not a single gesture or action is possible. Even when you appear to be fast asleep, a part of mind remains awake. This phenomenon is evident if a mosquito bites you during your sleep. Some part of your mind feels an itching sensation and your hand scratches the place where the mosquito has bitten you, even though you are not fully awake.

Every action you do has some motivation, conscious or unconscious, behind it. Not a single action can occur autonomously. You should never have to say you have done something but you don't know why you did it. It is important to understand why you are doing something and why you act the way you do. If you want to analyze and understand the motivation behind your actions, first you have to study your thought process. This is not so easy because the world within is subtler and more extensive than the world of actions. Whereas you can jot down your actions for the whole day in a few minutes' time, you cannot record one hour's thoughts, even if you try the whole day. It is no less difficult to count your thoughts than it is to count the stars. The thought process is like a river. One thought wave comes and goes, only to be immediately followed by another thought wave in the motion of the river of the mind.

Beneath the world of thoughts lies the world of emotions. You have been taught to try to regulate your actions and thoughts, but no one has taught you how to control your emotions. Emotions are more powerful than mind and can make you very sick or even destroy you. Even though you may be a highly cultured and intelligent person, one emotion can come and make you behave irrationally. For instance, you may lose your temper and behave in a totally unexpected manner. If you know how to work with emotional power, you can use it either destructively or creatively. If you cannot control your emotions, you will at least have to control your mind and thoughts. Then you can train the emotions by allowing them to go through the thinking process. Mind can help you to analyze why you become overly emotional because mind is a mirror. If you know how to calm down your mind, the mirror of the mind will reflect anything that is moving. But if emotions govern your mind, it is very difficult to study them.

Kama (desire)[1] is the ultimate motivation behind action. Therefore, you have to first contend with your desires if you want to understand the motivation behind your actions. The level of desire is deeper and more powerful than the emotional level. If you study your desires, it is easy to understand your life and the different aspects of your personality. Desire is karma in its most subtle form; emotion is karma in its most uncontrolled form. Action is thought, thought is emotion and emotion is desire. Therefore every action is virtually a thought, mingled with emotion and desire. So ultimately it is your desires that motivate you to act in the world.

You have not understood or tried to analyze what desires are or how to work with them. You don't question if you should allow a desire to motivate and direct your actions. You are only concerned in getting what you think you want, even though your wants and desires often go against your needs, as is evident in the following story:

One of the characters in the Ramayana epic, Kumbhakarna, was a great devotee and a very intelligent man. He was a huge man who had such an enormous appetite he could eat the food of the whole city for breakfast. So naturally everyone was disturbed when they learned he was praying to Brahma to grant him a boon: He wanted to be king of the gods.

---

1   Probably here the word *kama* means "desire" as one of the *purush-arthas: dharma, artha, kama* and *moksha,* the goals of human life.

All the human beings and even the gods became very worried when they came to know of his intentions. So Indrajit, the king of gods, went to Sarasvati, the goddess of wisdom, and pleaded, "Mother, we are in great need of your help. Please control his buddhi so that instead of saying he wants to be the king of the gods he will say he wants to be the king of sleep."

And thus it happened. When Kumbhakarna went to Brahma, Brahma said to him, "Tell me what you want."

When he spoke, the words came from his mouth that he wanted to be Nidrajit, the king of sleep.

Brahma said, "And that is exactly what is going to happen to you."

When Kumbhakarna realized his mistake, he cried. All of his brothers exclaimed, "Lord, what have you done?"

Brahma said, "I have not done anything. I had to give him whatever boon he desired. He asked to be the king of sleep so I have granted that boon to him. Okay, I will help you. Once in a year, he will wake up for one day."

If you perform an action, you have to reap the fruits of that action. This is the universal law of karma and it cannot be avoided. When an action, thought pattern, emotion or desire is expressed in the external world, you will reap the fruits of that particular expression. The law of karma is not something mysterious. Science, religion and philosophy all agree on the law of karma: *As you sow so shall you reap.* This is the law of karma as stated in the Bible. As we mentioned earlier, Newton's third law of motion is another expression of the law of karma.

No matter how much you pray, meditate or recite the bibles of the world, you still have to reap the fruits of your karma. The law of karma is inevitable. You cannot escape from doing your actions, no matter where you go or who you are. You have to continue to do actions, whether consciously, unconsciously or as a reaction. Whether you perform helpful or harmful actions, whether you think you are the worst or the best person, or whether you are a *sannyasi* or you live in the world, you are bound to receive the fruits of your karma. Negative karma will give you negative results and create obstacles for you; positive karma will help you in the process of enlightenment. You may reap the fruits of some actions very quickly, whereas others may take a long time. For example, if you sow the seeds of a flower, you will reap the fruits after one or two months. But if you sow the seeds of an apple tree, it will take many years before you can reap the fruits. In any case, if you do not sow the seeds skillfully, they will die and you will not reap the fruits at all. Only if you sow the seeds skillfully can you expect to reap the fruits.

You cannot separate karma, or cause, from the effect. Desire motivates you to do an action and when you perform the action you receive the fruits of that action. The action comes first, and then the fruits of the action — cause and effect. There is always a cause behind an effect; there is always an effect from a cause. As long as you do actions, you are bound to reap the fruits of those actions, and those fruits will again motivate you to do more actions. This is how actions create a whirlpool for you. There seems to be no end to it and no way to come out of it. Even though the best of your karma bears the best of fruits, you remain in the bondage of karma. If you perform karma without knowing why you are doing it, that karma will motivate you again and again, and you will keep repeating the same actions like a machine. In order to come out of this whirlpool and become master of your destiny, you have to know how to perform your actions so they do not affect you. Only when you understand the cause behind your actions can you have conscious control over your actions, because it is the cause that leads you to reap the fruits of your actions. Without rooting out the cause, you cannot control your destiny. If you trim a tree, after some time you will find that many branches are again growing out of the tree because the tree's roots are still there. You can only lead life perfectly once you remove the root cause. If you have been doing something that you know you should not do, the moment you become aware of this, stop doing it. The best repentance is not to repeat it. If you don't repeat it, it will die then and there and you will no longer reap the fruits of that action.

Karma is not limited to your present actions. There are three aspects of karma: past, present and future. Your karma encompasses all that you have done in the past, what you are doing now and what you are going to do in the future. If you understand how the past affects the present and the future and controls the river of life, you can solve the riddle of life. As a river flows spontaneously toward the ocean, making many curves and shaping many rocks, all human beings are flowing towards the ultimate reality, or perfection. The water ahead of you is flowing because there is a rush of water from behind pushing it forward. So is the case with karma. You see only the water that is rushing toward the ocean; you are not aware of the water that is behind you. If you think about your behavior, you will realize that you often don't know why you do the things you do and that you have been repeating the same mistakes again and again. This is because your behavior in the present is based on your previous experiences. Your present life and your future life are guided by the karma that you have already performed. The reservoir of your past karma is forcing you to do something now and will again force you to do something in the future.

Patanjali says you are not able to come out of the snare of karma because of the karma and kleshas that exist as deeply rooted latent seeds in the unconscious. Even though you may think you have done your duties, deep down there are certain karmas that are controlled by the kleshas stored in seed form in the unconscious. This is why, even if you may think you have finished with karma, suddenly again you find that you are being forced to do something that disturbs the whole course of your life.

Beneath your desires are the samskaras or impressions of your past karma. These samskaras, or strong motivations, that you have carried from your previous lifetimes or from your past, create bondage for you. Whatever you have done, the impression of that action dwells in the reservoir of the unconscious mind as a memory. Some of these impressions remain active and are known to you, and some have settled down in the latent part of your memory and you are not aware of them. It is easy to deal with the karma that you are aware of, but powerful, latent past karma can motivate you to behave in a manner that you don't understand. Those seeds that are deeply hidden in the reservoir of the unconscious are very strong and can suddenly come forward and create obstacles to your progress. Those samskaras can distract you, dissipate your energy, change the course of your life and disturb your willpower. If your samskaras are forcing you to do something, you cannot escape. If you try to resist them, you will only create more conflict for yourself. They will come and disturb you again and again because they are very strongly rooted in the unconscious. Without knowing your samskaras you cannot purify yourself or utilize the wisdom that you have stored from past lives or from your childhood. When those unknown seeds emerge from the basement, you become helpless and are not able to control yourself. But there is no need to brood on the past or think you cannot do anything about it. There is a way to deal with your samskaras. If you do your actions skillfully and selflessly and offer the fruits of your actions for others, you will get freedom. In this way you are going according to the law of karma and at the same time you are not creating bondage for yourself. Such action will lead you to a state of tranquility.

If the CAUSE Is Imperfect, the EFFECT Will Be Imperfect

The law of karma is applicable only to human beings. Nature fully governs animals, so they do not have free will. Unlike animals, humans have free will and thus are not under the control of anyone or anything external. If a person does not know how to use his free will then he lives exactly the way animals live, caught by the senses. If you do not understand how to use your free will, you are not fully utilizing your human resources. As a human being with free will, you have the power to control your actions and the capacity to think and decide what you want to do. You are responsible for your own destiny, even though you often try to put that burden upon God. Those who do not believe in the cycle of birth and rebirth say they are not responsible for any bad karmas and claim it is God who is to be held accountable because He created us. Without understanding what God is, you frequently say God has done this or that to you. God is the eternal, Self-existent reality that never changes in all times: past, present and future. Try to understand that God, the Lord of equality and love, would never cause you to suffer. Your suffering is the result of your own deeds. Don't allow yourself to be weak by using the excuse that your hardships have come from God. If you think like that, you cannot improve and there will be no joy in your life. You have free will. If you did not have free will, then you would be like a puppet or an animal. When you understand that your suffering is due to your own deeds, you will realize that your deeds have the power to shape your life. You are the architect of your life. As long as you believe that God has created you as you are, you will not feel it is possible to transform yourself. In addition, this philosophy brings up many questions: If God created you, and you had nothing to do with your birth, then God would have to be responsible for all of your actions and consequently would have to reap the fruits of your actions. You know it never happens like that. If you commit a crime, you go to jail, not God. If God were responsible for everyone's birth, how could you explain why some persons were born blind or with other defects? God is supposed to be impartial, so how could He have such discrimination? If He is not impartial, then He is not perfect. And if He is not perfect, what can He do for you if you are imperfect, and He is also imperfect?

People often claim they are suffering because it is God's will. What type of god would create you to make you suffer? Why should you love such a god and depend and rely upon him? If you say that some great power like God has created this world that is full of suffering, then He must be the most miserable of all beings. The real philosophy of life does not agree with this. The power that radiates God's love equally to all could never show favoritism toward some persons while making others suffer. Your suffering does not come from God, nor does God intervene in your actions. You create your own suffering, and then you pray to God to come down to help you. Don't try to dispose of your self-created problems or depend on a god who is outside you. If you were completely at the mercy of God, and God were doing everything for you, then it wouldn't matter if you did good or bad actions. There would be no need for you to worry about your karma or to pray or try to understand the mysteries of life. This philosophy is not helpful. The right philosophy says a human being is an unfinished being but has the capacity and opportunity to become complete and attain wisdom in this lifetime. No psychoanalyst, swami or yogi can help you if you do not help yourself.

Some claim everyone is born with sin. If you believe this is your first and only birth, how could you have brought sin with you? If God has created you, how could you be a sinner? This doesn't make any sense. If you believe you have come for the first time and will never come back, and the one who brought you here is controlling all your actions, thoughts, motivations and feelings, then why are you worried? If you think God has created you and therefore is responsible for all your actions and you don't have to do anything, then why do you have a mind to discriminate one thing from the other? Even though you may assert that God is controlling your life, you don't really allow God to do so. You want God to control your life the way you want it to be, so it's not really God but your wants that are controlling your life. You pray to God the way you want, and if God fulfills your mere wants, desires and needs, then you think He's a very good god and has answered your prayers. What is the purpose of praying, meditating and making self-effort, if God is controlling everything?

There are two worlds: the world manifested by God — the world of the sun, moon, stars and earth; and the world created by human beings. There is equality in God's manifestation. The great Lord of life loves all equally. The sun shines and the moon pales its light equally for all; the breeze blows for all and the rains are likewise impartial. Human beings have created a world over the world God has given. In the world human beings have created there is disparity. You have created partiality by your own thoughts and deeds. That is why you are suffering. The world of human beings is full of follies and mistakes, and is characterized by: *This is mine, and this is not mine.* This habit of possessiveness has established a world that is painful. Human beings have created such a world because they are imperfect. If the cause is imperfect, the effect will be imperfect. You have become imperfect because you have wandered far from the consciousness of the great Self to the physical, external self. The world you have created over the world manifested by God binds you; the world manifested by God does not. Your suffering is a superimposition you have created. You will have to seek freedom from the world you have created for yourself. The scriptures say you are suffering because of lack of knowledge and awareness of the One. In order to be free from suffering you have to follow two principles: maintain constant awareness of the eternal truth that is within you; and do your duties with love. Then you will be able to establish a bridge between the two worlds, the world within and the world without, and you will come to understand the mysteries of life.

The fact is there is no god who creates miseries for you nor who can remove your self-created miseries. You have to accept that all your suffering, pains and miseries are the result of your own actions. Don't blame anyone else. When you blame others it shows you are too weak to take responsibility for your own actions. This makes you dependent on others. I learned this lesson when I was young and lived in the jungles of Nainital:

When I was very young I lived in the forest and often would climb to the top of a tall tree and remain there for some time. When you leave your home you feel the joy of freedom but sometimes you can become a little irresponsible. During those days my willpower was very strong. I was very sensitive toward the pain of others, but not toward my own pain. I never cared if something happened to my body and would just mentally ask the pain to go away. The moment I thought that way, it would go.

Once I was enjoying myself sitting on the top of a tree that was more than thirty feet high. I had secured myself with another branch to keep from falling into the swampy lake that was just below the tree. I didn't realize the branch I was sitting on was not very strong. When I changed my position, the branch broke and I landed in the lake. It was one o'clock at night and very cold. I was trapped in swamp weed and didn't know what to do. I realized immediately I had created this painful situation and there was no one else to blame. Since I alone was responsible, I knew I had to make effort to come out of it. I kept trying to get free from that weed, but the more I tried, the more entangled I became, until gradually it had ensnared my whole body. Even though I was in agony, I was able to laugh at myself because I was very confident that I was not going to die. I kept making effort until finally I was able to break the snare of weeds around me and come out.

Many similar incidences happened to me when I lived in the jungle. Sometimes I had to go hungry and at other times I was in grave danger and came face-to-face with wild animals such as elephants and tigers. But I learned the whole key to survival was not to weaken myself.

At times I have also had the tendency to blame God for everything. But in moments of calm and clarity I realized it wasn't possible that God was responsible for my actions. I admitted I was committing mistakes and not using my intelligence. The law is: *As you sow, so shall you reap.* If I eat something bitter, God cannot create a sweet taste in my mouth. You can't believe in the law of karma, and at the same time think you are not responsible for your karma. It is erroneous to think you don't have to do anything because it all depends on God's grace and God will take care of everything. I will tell you a story of a swami who carried this belief too far:

Once there was a man who was very disappointed with life. He thought, *What is the use of doing things in the world? I want a car and a beautiful house but I don't have them. This life is not good. It's better to become a swami because swamis get everything without having to do anything. I will go to the Himalayas and dedicate everything to God. Then God will do everything for me.*

He had decided to tread the path of the Himalayas because he had heard the best swamis had been trained in that tradition. As he was walking he came upon a fig tree laden with beautiful, ripe figs. He wanted to have some but he was afraid he would be going against his vows if he picked the figs. So he lay down under that fig tree and thought, *God will drop the fig into my mouth. I don't have to do anything. I will eat the figs only if God gives them to me.* Then he opened his mouth, thinking that one of the figs would definitely fall into it. However, when the wind blew and a fig fell down, it fell to the ground by the side of his head. Another swami who was passing by saw him lying under the tree. He asked, "What is the matter with you? Why are you lying on the ground? Get up."

"No. God does everything, so I don't have to do anything. Why don't you just pick up a fig and put it into my mouth?"

The other swami said, "You foolish man. What kind of philosophy is this? You don't deserve to be wearing the garb of a swami. You have to do your part too. If the fig fell down by the grace of God, you should at least pick it up and eat it."

You often refer to the grace of God without understanding what grace is. I will explain it to you. Suppose you buy an orchard. You have to pay for the trees, the fruits and the land, but you don't have to pay for the shade. That is grace. There are two forces that function together. One is the ascending force or human effort, and the other is the descending force or grace. Human effort requires coordination of mind, action and speech. If you sincerely make effort, you will come in touch with the descending force or grace. When you are not successful in attaining something it means there was something wrong in your mind, action or speech. Don't put the blame on God. It may be that your mind was not one-pointed and you were not paying attention, or you have not trained the buddhi to decide on time. It could also be that you were not communicating clearly through your speech or actions. If you perform your actions skillfully, you are bound to get grace. When you feel all your resources are exhausted and no one in the world can help you, you cry with all your heart, "O God, please help me!" Then the door will open for you. That is grace. But if you become lazy and say, "I don't have to do anything. Let God give me His grace," you will never get grace. Laziness is the greatest sin for one who is on the path of enlightenment. Only when you have done your work sincerely does God's grace come. Atman reveals itself only to those whom it chooses. If you are among the chosen it means you have cultivated good qualities, made sincere effort and worked hard with yourself. Grace is the result of sincere effort. God's grace gives you the strength to face all the problems of life and the intelligence to perform your duties properly so you can get freedom from the bondage of karma.

The law of karma is very definite. Whoever you are, whether you are a religionist, philosopher or yogi, you are responsible for your own karma. You have to accept that your suffering is because of your own ignorance and not because of God or anyone else. You reap the fruits of all the actions you perform, and those fruits again motivate you to do fresh actions. You are not a dry leaf being tossed by the wind. If you commit a crime, you will be punished. You are in the bondage you have made for yourself, and you alone can liberate yourself from that self-created misery. You have vast resources and are capable of doing that. You have freedom to do your karma, but this means you also have to reap the fruits of your karma, not God. If you commit an act of violence, all the energy you use is His, but the violent act itself is yours and you will plunge into darkness. There can be no violence in the light of life; there is only light and love.

You are the architect of your life and thus have the capacity to change and shape your destiny. You choose what you want to be. One way to understand this is to think of yourself as an archer. The arrows you have previously shot are the past, and you cannot take them back. They are gone and will not be returned to you. You cannot undo the karma you have performed and you will have to reap the fruits of that karma. Even though you have no control over your past actions, you can have perfect control over the arrows that you have in your quiver and that you are shooting now. These represent the present. The arrows you are holding on your back and intend to shoot toward the target later correspond to the future. The past is gone, but what you do now and in the future is in your hands. The present is the link between the past and the future. If you keep thinking only of the past or imagining the future, you are missing the link of the present. You can change the whole flow of your life course if you live here and now and do your actions skillfully. This means to do them accurately, one-pointedly, sincerely, faithfully and with full devotion:

In ancient times students living in their gurus' houses, the *gurukulas,* were often tested. One of these tests was to ask them to collect and bring to their teacher some *kusha,* a grass considered sacred which is used in religious ceremonies. This grass is very sharp and cuts the hands if one is not skilled and careful when picking it. The students were divided into three levels based on their performance. The careless type of student hurried to pick up the grass because they had been ordered to get it. Since they were not careful, the grass cut their hands and fingers and they would bleed. Characteristic of another category were those students who were very lazy. They would not even go to cut the grass, but instead would ask others to get it for them. The third category was comprised of those students who were very skilled and knew the technique of pulling the grass carefully so it would not cut their hands. One who could pick that sharp grass without getting cut was called *kushala* (skillful). You have to be kushala when you perform your actions in the world.

Your life is duty-oriented. Anything you assume in your life is your duty. You were born in a particular family, country and society. You have to do your duties accordingly, taking full responsibility and working hard to carry out the duties you have assumed. Duties are of two types: those you do for yourself and those you perform for others. Your first duties are to yourself—to keep yourself clean, healthy and positive. Then you can look to your duties to others. Try to be loving and helpful to your family and friends.

You cannot live without doing your duties, but you should not allow them to make you a slave. When you do your duties but don't want to do them, you become a slave to them and they become a source of distraction, tension and stress. This happens when you are working in a job that is not suitable to you. You don't want to do it, yet you have to do it. This attitude creates constant internal conflict. If you generate interest in what you are doing, you will not create tension in your mind. The way to perform your duties so you do not become a slave to them is to do them with love. In this way you will not feel any boredom or tension, and they will not create bondage for you.

Many of my students complain that after getting married and having children, they no longer have time for meditation. Actually family life is also sadhana and everyone has to do this sadhana. Don't separate your duties from sadhana and the goal of enlightenment. Many people try to escape because they are afraid to face the problems in daily life, but there is no other way. You cannot get freedom from the bondage of karma by renouncing your karma. You may think you will become great if you renounce your marriage, duties and home and become a swami, but you cannot renounce your duties. You cannot enlighten yourself by discarding your relationships and duties, because the whole problem lies with the mind, not with the world. Wherever you go you carry your mind with you. To be a yogi means to live in the world and yet remain above it, wherever you are. You have to do your duties. Even if you feel disgusted with your duties, the solution is not to run away to a monastery. This is selfish, ego-centered behavior. If you become selfish and build boundaries around yourself, you will only suffer more. Your family and home make up your personal universe. The purpose of the family setup is to prepare you to deal with the rest of the world. In family life not only do you have to deal with your own anger, desires and needs, you also have to learn how to cope with the various temperaments and needs of the people in your family. Happiness comes from relationships. Even if you want to live all alone in the world, you will have to have a relationship with someone or something. Life means relationship. Freedom comes from giving, not from taking. If you give the fruits of your actions by offering them to your family and to the other people whom you love, your whole life will become a series of enjoyments. You suffer because you want to have all the fruits of your actions for yourself. You don't understand why you should give the fruits to others when you are the one who feels tired after doing your duties. When you are attached to the fruits, this creates not only problems such as greed, jealousy, pride and egotism, but also the motivation to do other actions that bind you even more. This is why it becomes more and more difficult to come out of bondage.

It is not necessary to go to any mountain retreat, temple, or swami or to stop doing your duties. If you dedicate the fruits of your actions to others, you can get freedom from the bondage of karma. Instead of expecting from others, see what you can do for them. Misery comes when you expect to receive without giving. If you give, you will definitely receive. The law of love is to give, not to take. If you practice the law of love you will become selfless, and then you will enjoy every moment of life. In love, you do everything for others without any expectation and you enjoy your duties; you give and you love to give.

If you do your duties skillfully, lovingly and happily, you will be doing your karma with the right attitude and you will be free.

The whole universe is a family, and we are all members of this family. Everyone should work for each other exactly as a family member works for the other members of the family. If everyone would work to help each other, all would become *jivan muktas* (liberated beings). Many people put a percentage of whatever they earn into a savings account thinking that the day might come when they will be sick and will need medical care. This means they are actually earning and preparing themselves for sickness. If you do that, you are directing your life toward sickness and uselessly keeping that fear in your mind. Instead you could be charitable and give something to someone who is sick now and needs help. Such a selfless act would give you great joy.

To do charitable work is considered to be one of the finest of all actions, provided you do it for the right reason. Unfortunately many people do charitable work to satisfy their egotistical whims. When you decide to help someone, selfishness and ego should not be involved. If you are doing something for someone, never expect anything in return. Otherwise, your real motive is to help yourself, not someone else. Rich people often do charity because they are afraid they might not get riches again if they don't share what they have, and also because they want name and fame. Some people want to do charity for the sake of their departed loved ones, while others give so they themselves will be benefited after death. Another reason for giving to charity is so others will say what a great person you are. But all of these are low levels of charity. Only a fortunate few do charitable work for the right reason. Those who understand the law of karma, do charitable work so they will be rewarded in their next lifetime. Charity done in this manner is definitely helpful in the path of enlightenment.

Give willingly and wholeheartedly to those whom you love, so that you do not become selfish. Charity should begin at home, but you should also find some way to do something selflessly for persons who are not related to you. Real charity comes when a person realizes he has so much he can share with those who do not have enough. When you hoard your wealth, you become selfish and egotistical and the progress of your growth is inhibited. It is better that you give what you have before somebody else or death snatches it from you. No matter how much you have to sacrifice, you should always look for ways in which you can do something for others without expecting anything in return. Just serve according to your ability and capacity. The whole process of life involves giving and giving. Give the best you have and you will definitely gain more.

Those who are considered to be great know how to perform their duties selflessly for humanity. They surrender the fruits of their actions to the Lord, whom they see in others. When you work for yourself, you are afraid you might not get the fruits, or if you get the fruits, perhaps they will be snatched from you. If you work for God, you will have no such fears and you will enjoy all the actions of your life. To serve others means to serve the Lord. If you could see God in those whom you love and do your duties for God, you would experience harmony and peace within. You could never hurt or treat someone badly if you could see God in that person. When a swami sees another swami he calls, *"Namo Narayan,* which means "I bow to Narayana, to God in you." The other swami likewise responds, "Namo Narayan" (I also bow to God within you). Both are aware of one reality. When you do your duties selflessly you come to understand God through others. A human being is a mirror that can introduce you to God. When you love the highest One who is in everyone, external form disappears and reality alone exists. Patanjali says one of the finest ways to obtain freedom is to give all the fruits of your work and surrender yourself to the Lord.

Karma will continue to bind you if you do your actions for yourself. If you renounce the fruits of your karma, but continue to do your karma, that karma will not bind you. If you do your karma skillfully and selflessly for others, then others will reap the fruits of your actions. When your mind, action and speech become spontaneously directed toward selflessness, you are on the path toward freedom. The highest of all prayers is to do your duties with love. In this way you will not be giving something to another human being; you will be giving to the Lord who is in every human being. That is prayer through action or karma. Through prayer you may be inspired and you may get the strength to face the results of all the deeds you have done in the past, but prayer will not liberate you. Prayer can help you to strengthen your determination so that you do not perform those karmas that create barriers for you.

Selfless service, done lovingly and skillfully, is real prayer. It is the highest form of worship and can help you to liberate yourself from the bondage of karma. Through selfless action you can express your love to others. When selfless service becomes habitual, you no longer live for yourself or for sense gratification. When you do your actions for the purpose of knowing the ultimate truth, they become acts of worship. Discharge your duties skillfully and selflessly, and surrender the fruits of your actions to the Lord within. Then you will be working as a representative of the Lord.

The difference between a great man and one who is not great is this: A great man does everything selflessly for others; a small, petty man, who lives like a creature in this world, does all things for himself. Karma done with selfish desire or motivation will produce bondage; karma without any desire or purpose will not. One who has no motivation, even if he continues to do karma, that karma will have no effect on him. When the pot maker has finished making a pot, the wheel continues to rotate, even though it does not produce anything. So is the case with karma. In the case of true renunciates, karma has no binding effect because they don't perform those karmas that are binding. Likewise, karma does not affect those who are enlightened. The fruits never affect a great man because he has surrendered them to others. Such great persons live on the earth as free beings, serving others and helping others to become aware of the reality. For those who are liberated, death and birth do not create problems because they are under their conscious control. If they want to be born again, they will do so to serve others.

This freedom will come when you understand the whole process within and without. First, you should learn to be an insider, and then how to be happy and to behave and express yourself in the external world. For this you should follow certain principles: Remember that the things of the world are for you to use, but you should not become attached to them. Don't forget you are on a journey and are only a guest in this world. Next, do your karma according to your ability and surrender the fruits of your actions for the Lord. Enjoy the act of surrendering the fruits of your actions; do not do it out of frustration or out of a sense of having been forced to do it. Always maintain awareness in your daily actions. And finally, pray to the Lord of life to give you the strength to follow the right path. Then, even if you commit mistakes, it doesn't matter because you are following the path of truth.

There was one great poet who prayed to God, "Lord, help me to understand the purpose of life. O God, why do all these opposites exist? Somewhere there is pain, somewhere joy, somewhere happiness, somewhere unhappiness, somewhere rain and somewhere drought. What is all this? You have the power to stop all these opposites in life. Why do I feel joy, but my neighbor is unhappy and crying? You are the Lord of the universe. You can change all this."

Another poet said, "You are a fool. This world exists only because opposites exist."

The third said, "You both have simply understood there are mysteries, but you have not known the solution."

They asked, "What is the solution?"

"Pray to God to give you inner strength so you can go through this procession of life comfortably."

Inner strength does not come from selfishness. The more selfish you are, the weaker you become. Any time you feel you should receive something for your deeds it is a selfish act. When you have no personal involvement in any way and you do your actions for others, you will feel great joy.

To live and function in the external world is only a small aspect of your life. You should have a goal in your life to reach and there should be no conflict between your duties and this goal. The purpose of being born and living in the world is to accomplish the final goal of realization of the absolute truth. Conflict comes when you indulge too much in the enjoyments of the world and forget the goal of life. You want to be successful in the external world, but you have not properly interpreted what success is. Suppose you have two million dollars and five houses. This kind of success is not healthy if it is not related to the goal of life. Please don't misunderstand and think I am telling you not to have desires. The goal of life is not to be desireless. Rather you should have desires, but not for selfish purposes. You need only one powerful and burning desire to lead your mind inward to know the absolute reality. The highest desire is the desire to know your Self.

When I visited Gandhiji's ashram in my childhood with Ramdasji, his son, we used to find a few moments to sit with him. On one of these occasions I asked him, "Sir, how can one easily attain moksha or liberation?" Gandhiji said, "Gradually reduce your desires. When you have reduced them to the zero point, you will be free."

Desires create bondage for you. You can either fulfill all your desires or renounce them. When you have only one desire — the desire to give — then you will be living for others, not for yourself. When you do not live for yourself, then also you will die for others, and death will no longer terrify you. You will understand that death is only a habit of your body and you can enjoy life. Those who do not enjoy life here can never enjoy life hereafter.

You are the architect of your life and you can unfold all the hidden pages of life. You can understand the depth of your being and you can attain that which is not fathomable by the ordinary mind. The moment you come to know who you really are, you will rise above your destiny. You can do this if you follow certain guidelines:

• Never condemn yourself for what you have done in the past or think that you are bad or guilty of having committed many sins. The only sins are the obstacles you create for yourself. If you don't repeat what you have done in the past, you will not create any more obstacles.

• You shouldn't do anything for which you will have to repent.

• By doing your actions under conscious control, you can become master of your actions.

• Your actions should always have a definite purpose. If the purpose is missing, you will not do them wholeheartedly and instead will be doing them merely as a pastime. Live your life in a disciplined way and use your energy according to the purpose you have fixed in your life.

• Remember that your foremost duty is to become aware of the kingdom of Atman. All your actions should have the final goal of Self-realization. For this you need constant awareness of the reality in your daily life.

• And finally, you should understand that all the fruits of karma are perishable, not everlasting.

The law of karma is simple: right thought, right speech and right action. If you perform your duties properly, you will experience perennial happiness. When you form the habit of constant awareness of the reality, and that habit becomes part of your unconscious, then all motivations will lead you toward right actions. This will give you freedom and help you to enjoy life and to understand the purpose of life. You all want to attain samadhi, a state of peace, bliss and happiness, and freedom from all pains. You can do this by doing your actions lovingly and selflessly. You may think I am talking about something that is beyond you, but it is very practical and realistic. To attain enlightenment does not mean to receive something nor is it the result of taking drugs. Enlightenment means freedom from the misery and bondage you have created. Even if you feel that you are lost and have committed many mistakes, and you don't know how to do it, just start to practise. The simplest way is to serve the people with whom you live. We all can help to create happiness in this world by serving others selflessly according to our capacity. That is the greatest of all prayers. The more selfless you become, the closer you come to a higher level of life. You have to be free from three bondages: karma, fear and ignorance. If all individuals would do their karma lovingly and selflessly for others, humanity would attain a new height.

Don't take your karma lightly. Your karma creates your destiny here and hereafter and is responsible for your birth. You are going round and round through the series of births and deaths because of the law of karma. If you transform your personality, there will be no karma.

If you are tied with a rope and I burn that rope, a trace of the rope will remain but it will have no power to tie you. Likewise, karma will still be there, but it will have no power to bind you. Once you are free from the bondage of karma you can create your own destiny.

There are two shores of life: life here and life hereafter. A river flows between the two shores. Wise is he who has knowledge of this shore and the other shore — lower knowledge and higher knowledge. Lower knowledge leads you to success in the world; higher knowledge leads you to liberation. There is no need to renounce the world. The sages say you need both. Once you have knowledge of both shores of life here and hereafter, all doubts will vanish, and the binding impact of karma will be destroyed.

ALL OF LIFE Is a Long Procession from ETERNITY to Eternity

There are four basic questions in life:

Who am I?

From where have I come?

Why have I come?

And where will I go?

Life is like a manuscript in which the beginning and end are missing. You are aware of the middle portion, the segment between the two points of birth and death, but that is only a small sentence in the book of life. Humanity is still primitive in that there are only a fortunate few who have understood the meaning of life here and hereafter. You know you are here, but you do not know from where you have come, why you have come to this world or where you will go after this life.

An explanation of the cycle of reincarnation can help you to understand how you are here. Although you have no recollection of what happens between death and birth, you can comprehend what is meant by rebirth and how you are reborn. Birth and death are two doors. You come in from the door of birth and go out through the door of death, where you remain hidden until you come forward again through another birth. So birth and death are simply two changes in the cycle of reincarnation.

The question comes: *What is the proof there is rebirth?* Your presence here is proof that you were somewhere else before. Otherwise you wouldn't be here now because you could not have come from nothing. There is no such thing as a heap of dirt that God uses to create more and more people. First you were there and then you came here. You are a citizen of two worlds. One is known, and the other is unknown to you. Your very presence here also indicates that eventually you will go somewhere else because you have come from somewhere else. After this life in the known world, you will die and again go back to the unknown. For some time after death you will remain hidden, and then you will again come forward.

Next you want to know *how* you have come to this world, and if anyone has forced you to come. Sometimes you feel unsatisfied with life and you grumble because you think you were pushed to come to this world by some unknown power. If this were true, you would be no different than a puppet. You wouldn't be responsible for your actions nor could you determine your own course of life. The fact is neither God nor anyone else is responsible fro your birth. Birth is not an accident. You don't come all of a sudden and you are not left to fate. There is nothing like luck, chance or predestination. If you believe in destiny, there is no place for human will. Fate simply means that which you have done in the past. Since you are the creator of your past, you have made your own fate. As a human being you create your own destiny and you have the power to change the course of your destiny.

However you cannot come all of a sudden without any reason. When you leave this world you carry with you the burden of unfulfilled desires. It is that burden that motivates you to come back. But desire is also the mother of many problems. Some desires are helpful while others are obstructive to your growth. For example, if you desire to eat nutritious and wholesome food to keep your body healthy so it can become an instrument for Self-realization, that desire is helpful. But many desires are injurious to you and become obstacles on the path. And once you fulfill one desire, thousands of others follow. That is why one lifetime is not sufficient for all the experiences you must have to fulfill all your desires. If you start something today and cannot complete it, you finish it tomorrow. Death is like a prolonged sleep. When you wake up, you again start doing the same things you did not complete in your previous lifetime. This continues until you complete yourself and attain that for which you have come. The philosophy of reincarnation assures this is not your only life.

The body, breath and conscious mind are your vehicles to experience the known world. After death, your unconscious mind and individual soul are your vehicles in the unknown. You come back to this world again and again because your unconscious mind, the vehicle your individual soul is driving, carries all the samskaras and unfulfilled desires from your previous lives. Desire is the motivation for rebirth. The unfulfilled desires of your previous lives motivate your life force to project forward and bring you back to this platform again. Those desires lead you toward a certain path. Just as you have certain desires to fulfill in this lifetime before you drop your body, you will assume a body again to fulfill incomplete karma and unfulfilled desires in your next lifetime. As long as you have a desire, you will have to come back to fulfill that desire. If you continue to be tossed by more and more desires you will have to be born again and again to fulfill those desires. You cannot fulfill your desires in dreamland; you have to fulfill them right here and now with feeling and sensing.

Suppose you have a beautiful house and family and you are lamenting because you know you are dying and will no longer be able to enjoy them. When you go to the other world, you will carry with you a deep impression of that house and your family. When you are reborn you search for your previous family, and they search for you. You meet each other again and you know each other very well. So this world is not new to you. You have previously known the people with whom you are living now. You chose them unconsciously and they likewise chose you. The surroundings in which you were reborn — the country, place, family and community — were your choice. For example, I am the way I am and I was born in India in the Himalayas because I had a great desire, and I still have, to be born in the Himalayas. If I am to be born again, I will be born in the Himalayas because I carry that desire with me in my unconscious.

It was also your choice as to what body you would take on in your next life. You chose the color and type of garment you wanted to wear and that's what you got. Whatever you are, it was all your choice. Even those persons who have a life full of sorrow have chosen it, because they did not know any other way. The choices you make are based on your previous experiences. Now you are trying to escape from something you have chosen for yourself. It is better to be wiser before you choose. Although you are not satisfied with the known, you are afraid to leave the known and go to the unknown. This is the self-created misery of humanity today. Self-created miseries are the greatest obstacles in life.

If you analyze how you are suffering, you will realize all of your sufferings are because of your own actions. Though you may have everything, still you may feel sad inside. This is one of the signs and signals of spiritual thirst that may lead you to seek within. Maybe your sufferings have come from the past; maybe you are suffering because you don't understand who you are, from where you have come, why you have come or what the purpose of your life is. But you can solve those questions. Even if you don't remember from where you have come and you don't know where you will go, you are here. If you study this life you can find the answers to those questions.

What you were yesterday, that you are now. What you make of yourself now is what you will become tomorrow. You have individuality because you wanted it, and you have a particular personality because of your habits. The word *persona* means "mask." No one has given you this mask to wear; you are playing a particular role because you wanted to do that. You cannot continue to do something for a long time if you are not meant to do it. You are not meant to do that which you have not practised before. If you are meant to be a drummer, you will not be able to play the piano with the same perfection. Likewise, if you are meant to be a vocal musician, you cannot become a ballet dancer. You can develop another talent alongside your main talent, but you will not be able to perfect it.

You are like a musician who creates his own symphony. When you understand the rhythms of life within you, you will become a great musician. All the music of the world has the same seven keynotes. You also have seven keynotes, or seven levels of consciousness. If you want to sing, it will come from the level of consciousness where you are. If you have gone deeper within to a higher level, you will create your music from somewhere else. The great musicians who have charmed the world were able to do so because they had gone to that height.

You are what you were before, but you can become whatever you want to become. If you desire something, you will have it. Whatever you have has come to you because of your desires. Nothing happens without your having desired it, whether that desire was conscious or unconscious. This is all your doing. You simply are not aware of it. Once you become aware of it, the whole mystery of life will be solved.

You have come from the unknown to the known, from the unseen to the seen. That is birth. In the Sanskrit language there are three expressions used for birth: *janma, janih pradurbhava* and *utpatti.* That which has come from the unknown, unseen world, is called *srishti.* Before you came to this world you were dormant in the unknown like a seed. There cannot be birth without death. A seed has to break and die before it can grow and become a plant. The seed represents the unknown part of life; the plant is the known part. If you understand how a tree can come from a tiny seed, you can understand the philosophy of reincarnation. Just as the plant carries the seed, the seed carries within itself a potential plant. A tree comes out of a seed, and then it bears more seeds. Before the seed sprouts and grows into a tree, it has to germinate in the subtle world. A tree may die, but its seeds survive. Similarly, when the body dies, the seed or the soul continues to exist.

Though the conscious mind fails when you drop your body and breath, your unconscious mind, the reservoir of merits and demerits and desires and feelings, acts as the vehicle for your individual soul. Merits help you and inspire you to grow and to unfold; demerits create hurdles or obstacles in the path of enlightenment.

To come out of the seed is birth; to go back to the seed of life is death. Your very existence proves that you have come from the unknown world, you are going to return to the unknown and after some time you will again come back. That is rebirth. Reincarnation means you have come from the unknown to the known, and again you will go back from the known to the unknown. There was something before this and there will be something beyond this.

If you understand reincarnation, you will understand karma, because reincarnation supports the law of karma. This world is the field of action. If you sow a seed today, you will not reap the fruits of your sowing tomorrow. It takes time. If you understand that you will reap the fruits of whatever you have done in the past, then you can do something that will help you to attain enlightenment. I witnessed a very interesting event in my youth that reinforced the philosophy of reincarnation:

Because I often used to travel from place to place on the banks of the Ganges, many people knew me in the cities that are situated there. Sometimes I would stay with someone for a few days and then again travel. Once during rainy season I was staying in the guesthouse of the district magistrate in the city of Ghazipur. He was very disturbed about something strange that had just happened. He said to me, "There is a ninety-six year old *sadhu* who never wears anything, no matter what season it is. We have observed him and have found that he is very sincere in his austerities. He sleeps for one half-hour only and the rest of the time he sits in meditation. But recently he did something very odd. He rushed over to a woman who was taking her bath in the Ganges and started to suck her breasts. The people who were nearby and had witnessed this gave him a good beating. He was jailed for this crime and the case went to court. The judge in the court was a disciple of this swami and he did not know what to do. He knew the swami very well but many people had witnessed this odd behavior of the swami, so there was nothing he could do. The judge said, 'He is my teacher. I want this case to be transferred.'

"The people insisted, 'No. You have to do it.'

"I was in the courtroom when they brought him in for the trial. He walked in like the lord of the world. He was there, yet he was not there. The judge offered him a chair and he sat. He immediately asked the judge, 'Why have you put me in jail? Why are these people doing this to me? That woman was my mother. She used to breastfeed me and then she stopped all of a sudden. So I had a right to do what I did.'

"Everyone was shocked. Finally someone said, 'You are *paramahansa*. It is not the tradition of paramahansas to have long hair. Why do you have long hair?'

"He made a quick motion with his hand, and the hair of everyone in the courtroom fell off. I witnessed this. Then he said, 'I will burn everybody here into ashes if anybody doubts my dignity. What do you mean by saying I am not paramahansa? I have spent my whole life in training myself and today you say I am not what I have been doing?'

"When he looked at the inspector of police, that man started to shake because of the current he was experiencing. Then the sadhu said, 'Call that woman and ask her if she is my mother. That's all.'

"The woman came in and he asked her, 'Are you not my mother? Just say one word.'

"When she looked at him she remembered her past life. She remembered she had become very ill and was no longer able to feed her child. When she died, he was left alone. She remembered the whole thing and started to cry. Finally she admitted, 'Yes, you are my child.'

"The court did not know what to do with all this because there were no legal facts on which to base any decision. The only fact they could see was that when he made a certain gesture, everyone's hair fell off. He was acquitted honorably."

Reincarnation is not some absurd idea of a crazy thinker. Christianity does not promote the doctrine of reincarnation because Christ did not discuss it in the Bible. Yet Christians expect Christ to come again. That is reincarnation. Nowhere is it mentioned in the Bible that Christ instructed his disciples not to believe in reincarnation. All the great faiths during that period professed reincarnation. It was a common and simple philosophy and everybody believed in it. I don't care whether reincarnation is believable or not. I do not believe in reincarnation; I know it. Belief systems come through indirect knowledge; realization comes through direct knowledge. I do not believe, but I know that the philosophy of karma and reincarnation is valid. Reincarnation is a law of life, but you should not believe in it because I tell you. You should know it.

Whether you believe in reincarnation or not, it's not a big thing. I found out with the guidance of my master that it's not necessary to know about your past lives because it can create a great disturbance in your present life. You might have been a killer in the past and today you are a sage, or maybe you were a fool in the past and now you are wise. If you were to come to know these things, what would happen to your wisdom now? To know the past will not make you creative. If you think too much about reincarnation, you will be wasting all of your energy in the grooves of past memories:

Tagore was a great poet from the East. He had a large institute called Shantiniketan, which is a renowned university now. When I was a student there, I met Lama Govinda who was teaching there during those days. There was another person who had accompanied him and when I met that person I felt that I had known him very well in a previous life. I kept quiet because feeling is only feeling, and you cannot rely on it. When I was on vacation, I went to my master and I said, "I want to know who I was before this life."

He said, "If you really want to know your past, just do this meditation practice and after one week's time you will come to know your past lives."

When I start something, I do it until I complete it, no matter what happens. I don't eat or sleep and I don't talk to anyone. I just sit down and do it. So I started the practice, and after seven days a great confusion came into my life. I began to recognize people I had definitely known before. There was no question in my mind. But they did not recognize me, so I became very frustrated. When I would meet someone who had been a friend of mine in the past, I would say, "How are you?"

That person would not even look at me. And when I met someone who had been my enemy, I felt afraid of him. Everything came together — past, present and future — and my mind started to become imbalanced because I didn't know how to deal with it all. This could happen to any student. Actually I had started to recall my previous life from the age of two years. I remembered the place where I had previously lived and the people with whom I had lived. I kept telling my family, "I don't belong to this house and village, and I don't belong to you."

One day they asked, "To whom do you belong and where is your place?"

I told them I was born at such and such place on such and such date. So they took me to that place and I recognized everything and told them the names of the people I had known there. I didn't want to leave that village. This happened when I was only two years old. Gradually I forgot, and by the age of four I had only a faint idea of my past. One day I met my mother of a previous life. She was very young and I was grown up. When we met it was difficult for people to separate us. Those who were witnesses decided to test me to see if anyone had coached me to behave in that manner or if my behavior was authentic. I was able to answer all the questions they asked. Now I remember my past lives as clearly as I remember this life. There is no difference.

I have demonstrated to my students, to those who practise, how it is possible to know the past, present and future. For a yogi who has learned how to have control over his mind and modifications, to know the past and the future is very easy. There is one method of meditation that can take you back several lives in the past, but this is a sheer waste of time. You are not the same person you were in the past. Even now you are changing every second, so there is no purpose in being so enticed with the past.

Your mind has been conditioned by the past, present and future. If you can get freedom from these conditionings, you will be able to peek into the future very easily, because it is mind that has built the boundary between the present and the future. Your mind has the tendency to either think of the past or jump to the future. Actually, past, present and future are only events of the mind. There are many events going on, but time is different from events, just as the flowing river is different from the riverbed. Life is a series of events. Beneath all these events there is something subtler. Today and tomorrow are events, not time. Your whole life is eventful, but there is only one time, and that is eternity.

Though you talk of the present, you never experience it because you do not know how to enjoy here and now. Learn to experience the present and enjoy every moment here and now, because that is perennial joy. That awareness can be retained with the help of meditation, because meditation is a bridge between the other shore and this shore. Only prayer and meditation can lead you to here and now.

Knowledge alone can liberate you from the fears of birth and death. Ignorance creates fears and that is why you suffer. Slowly expand your knowledge of here and hereafter, of the known and the unknown. When you understand the mysteries of birth and death, you will realize that nobody was responsible for your birth and nobody will be liable for your death.

If you understand where a river appears from and where it disappears to, you can understand the philosophy of reincarnation. All the rivers flow toward the ocean. With so much water continuously rushing into the ocean, it seems there would be great floods that would destroy the whole world. This does not occur because the water of the oceans keeps changing its form. It evaporates, then condenses and again falls down as water; or it solidifies and becomes ice, which melts and again becomes water. Nothing happens to water; it simply changes its form to vapor or ice. The same is true for the individual soul. At death, the individual leaves the physical body and continues life in the energy body. You are not something new, nor did you come to this platform without a purpose.

When you leave this world you carry all of your experiences with you in the unconscious mind. Some time after death, you will again use that vehicle to come back and be born again. You assume a body and a conscious mind again and again to become perfect, eternally happy and full of wisdom and peace. You keep coming back to fulfill this purpose, but instead you are repeatedly caught by your actions and senses. Because of ignorance you separate yourself from the whole and you are not able to complete the purpose of your life. This goes on. If you can get freedom from this cycle, you will become one with the cosmos, exactly like a drop of water meets the ocean and becomes the ocean. As long as you are afraid of losing your individuality, it is not possible. In order to go forward you will have to get rid of that fear and accept the Universal Self. When you unite the individual soul with the Cosmic Soul, you will be free. Death means separation; union means life.

Whether you believe in reincarnation or not, you still have to make progress here and you have to accept the law of karma. You have desires that you want to fulfill and you work with all your might to fulfill them. Those desires motivate you to do actions, which again prompt you to do more actions. In this way you remain caught. Your desires are still there after you drop your body and even when you assume another body. As long as you have desires, there can be no liberation. There will no longer be motivation for rebirth once you have fulfilled all your desires.

Ordinary people take rebirth because they have desires to fulfill in the world. There are also great persons who choose to reincarnate because they have a selfless desire to serve others. Such persons who are enlightened do not suffer from individual karma for they are not doing karmas for themselves. Though they are here with us, they have a higher purpose of living in the perennial truth. Truth is timeless. Those who live in truth are free from time, space and causation and the cycle of past, present and future.

The cycle of birth and death will continue as long as you choose to be an individual and you have desires. You will remain on this particular plane of consciousness as long as you are caught up by the charms, temptations and attractions of the world. The moment you become aware that there is a higher level of consciousness there will be no question of renouncing this particular level. You will be here, though you are there. This technique is called doing your duties in the world, yet remaining above.

Patanjali says it is necessary to understand the twin laws of karma and reincarnation. As you do karma you reap the fruits because the cause is there. If you are not free from the cause, you cannot stop yourself from reaping the fruits. When you have a desire to fulfill, you have to come back to the world to fulfill that desire. Reincarnation is a must in order to get freedom from karma, but you can get freedom from reincarnation also.

There are two aspects of life: the known and the unknown. One who is ignorant knows only the known aspects of life: the body, senses and conscious mind. You can get freedom from suffering by knowing both the known and the unknown. When you are no longer satisfied with the world and become aware that there must be something beyond this phenomenal world, you will feel the necessity to know the unknown part of life and you will question life: *Whose mind, whose body and whose senses are these? Who is conducting my mind?* Then you will come to know there is something called the individual soul. More questions come: *How is the individual soul related with all other souls? How are the individual soul and other souls related to the Absolute One?*

If you collect all the souls from all the human beings and creatures in the world and put them together, the accumulation is God. All fears go away when you realize God exists everywhere. I'm afraid of you or you're afraid of me because we think we are different from each other. You're afraid and insecure because you think there is someone apart from you who exists. The teachings say there is only one absolute, indestructible, immeasurable infinite truth without second. The more you remember the one absolute truth that is within and without, your fears will eventually vanish.

Those who are wise know we have come from eternity, we are in eternity and we will go back to eternity. Though we have individual form, we all come from the same ocean. The ocean is in continuous motion, moving forward and then withdrawing itself. This motion of expansion and contraction is the very law of life. When a wave rises we call it birth, and when it falls we call it death. Nothing happens to the ocean when a person is born, lives in this world and again goes back to eternity. Therefore there is no need to mourn. As long as we are not conscious of the ocean we remain as little waves; when we become conscious of the ocean, we become the ocean. The moment a person comes to know the unknown part of life, he knows the ocean beneath all the waves, the One who is manifested in all, and is free. He has no fear of death or fear of losing something because he knows the known and the unknown parts of life. The center of happiness is within. When you are able to still the waves of the lake of the mind, you will find that happiness.

Only those who are wise have access to the mysteries of death and birth. Death and birth are two gates. If you go through one, you will come out through the other. It depends on your desires. Those who are wise have become weary of these rounds of births and rebirths. If you want to serve your people or the suffering masses, you can do it. If you decide to remain in the ocean of bliss, you can also do that. You are an ancient traveler who keeps coming and going in this world. All of life, from birth to death and back to birth again, is a long procession from eternity to eternity. If you live here and now, you can expand your consciousness and get freedom from the snares of life and death. This is the philosophy of reincarnation.

A Tranquil, SATTVIC Mind
Is the HIGHEST Mind

Up to this point we have considered the kleshas and the vrittis, but we have not mentioned the *gunas*. Patanjali says it is essential to get freedom from the conflicts within and without that arise from the gunas and the vrittis. Even in your longing for the highest purpose, you will have conflicts. To know the nature of your mind, you have to study the various vrittis or modifications of the mind, which are described in the first pada, and also be able to recognize which particular guna is influencing and controlling your mind and life. *Guna* is a Sanskrit word which means "quality." There are three gunas or qualities of the mind: *rajas, tamas* and *sattva*. You can easily determine which of the three gunas is predominant if you sit quietly and study the state of your mind. Sometimes in meditation you may see waves of colors. The colors you are visualizing indicate which guna is predominant or active.

When your mind is very active in doing things or trying to attain something in the world, it is under the influence of rajas. Your mind remains very active the whole day, trying to fulfill mundane desires without understanding why it is doing so. The mind can be negatively active or positively active when it is rajasic. If you are selfish and working for yourself, the mind is considered to be negatively active. When it is positively active, you can successfully do what you want to do. The color of rajas is always red. If you want to know if you are under the influence of rajas, just sit down and close your eyes. If rajas is dominant you will immediately have an image of red light.

Tamas means "overcome by inertia in habits, thoughts, speech and behavior." When tamas is excessive you tend to do negative things that hurt yourself or others. Under the influence of tamas, mind is controlled by sloth and laziness and finds excuses to avoid doing anything. Everyone has the quality of tamas to some extent, but when it is excessive it can be very harmful. When this is the case your animal nature surfaces and you become selfish, inconsiderate, get angry easily and tend to hurt and harm others. You prolong your sleep to eight to ten hours, wake up and work only for yourself, not for others. This is the way animals behave. Tamas is associated with darkness and the color black.

Karma is a law. You cannot live without it, no matter how lazy you are. If you are tamasic, you will receive the fruits of tamas; if you are rajasic, you will receive the fruits of rajas; and if you are sattvic, you will receive the fruits of sattva.

If you find you are too rajasic or tamasic, there is no need to cry or condemn yourself. The purpose of studying the qualities of the mind is to make you aware of what you need to do to train yourself. Whether the mind is overactive or too passive, it needs training to overcome all negative habits.

Sattva gives tranquility, equanimity and peace to the mind. Under the influence of sattva guna, your mind is peaceful, and you feel love for everybody. The sattva guna is associated with light and its color is clear white. A tranquil, sattvic mind is the highest of minds and is never disturbed no matter what happens.

At this point I would like to clarify that those who meditate or pray frequently are not all sages and are not necessarily sattvic. For example, two characters of the Ramayana, Ravana and Rama, were both considered great persons and great devotees, but they were very different. Ravana was a very learned Brahmin king and Rama was a prince. Ravana was acceptably a greater scholar than Rama and came from a Brahmin family, while Rama was not from a Brahmin family. He did not have that traditional background where mother and father educate the child from the very beginning. Though they were both great devotees of Lord Shiva, Ravana used to spend many hours in meditation and had attained many *siddhis* (supernatural powers) as a result of his devoted practices. Rama had not attained siddhis.

But nobody loves or remembers Ravana today. It is Rama who is the object of everyone's devotion. This is because Ravana was very selfish. He wanted to be supreme and even resorted to killing others so he could attain that status. This is why he was known as the king of demons. He prayed to Lord Shiva with great devotion and sincerity and therefore received many boons from him, one of which was to become a great warrior. The *devas* (bright beings), who were the highest beings during that time, did not know how to deal with him. On the other hand, Rama was known as the prince of peace, truth and happiness. The nature of his mind was pure sattva, and so he was beloved by all, and still is today.

The goal of humanity is to attain that culture where the whole universe becomes a family, and everyone feels love for each other. To feel love for each other means to feel love for the Lord. In order for this to happen, everyone will have to acquire a state of mind in which the quality of sattva is predominant. To be spiritual means to awaken sattva in your life.

The Very Root of the ASHTANGA System Is
ATTENTION

Now we come to ashtanga yoga, Patanjali's systematic and scientific method to attain samadhi. *Ashta* means "eight;" *anga* means "limbs." Patanjali describes the eight limbs of yoga as eight rungs or steps of a ladder. Every step is independent yet sequential. The purpose of each step is to make you aware of and prepare you for a higher step of life.

Ashtanga yoga is more commonly known as raja yoga. When he was in the West, Swami Vivekananda coined the term *raja yoga* for the convenience of westerners. The word *raja* means "royal." The path of raja yoga, or ashtanga yoga, leads you systematically from the gross to the subtle, from the subtle to the subtler and from the subtler to the subtlest aspects of your being. This is the final destination, the royal palace in the deep recesses of the inner chamber of your being, where His Majesty dwells. If you follow the path of ashtanga yoga as Patanjali has prescribed, you will be able to verify that your true nature is divine and realize your fullest potential for creative thought and action.

Ashtanga yoga encompasses teachings from many different paths. These are revealed teachings of divine origin that go back many thousands of years. Through the practical methods of ashtanga yoga you can achieve mastery of all three realms—physical, mental and spiritual—and full realization of the Self. At present you are only aware of your mortal self. The knowledge that you are a mortal self, having a body, breath, conscious mind and unconscious mind, does not help to transform your personality. Self-realization means you have realized the center of consciousness, the Self-existent truth that is within. There is no need to search in the external world or to go to any temple, mosque or church. Self-realization is the expansion of your individual soul to cosmic consciousness. For knowing the Self you will have to systematically tread the internal journey deep into the inner chamber of your being. You have two levels of energy or power; one is asleep and one is awake. If you remain asleep, you will always be weak. You can easily awaken and use those powers creatively and expand the field of the conscious mind until there is no longer anything unconscious. Then you will be able to consciously bring forward whatever knowledge you want from the infinite library within for use in your daily life. Those great sages who walked on the earth like Christ, Moses and others, were human beings like us. They became great because they knew how to use the infinite library within.

Millions of people tread this path, but only a fortunate few persist to complete the journey. This is because you are confused about what you are seeking. You say you are searching for God, but if He were to suddenly come and ask you what you want, many of you would ask Him to give you a new car, or a good boyfriend or girlfriend. And if God were to ask you who you are, you would only be able to respond that you don't know. In order to meet the president, you will also have to be a president. If you go as a beggar, his attendants will tell you to get out because the president has no time to meet a beggar. But if you go as a president, he will come out and graciously receive you.

Ashtanga yoga is considered to be a very good path for everyone, especially for those who want to understand the true value of life with its currents and cross currents. On this path even though you will definitely meet many obstacles, you will also encounter many milestones to indicate how much progress you have made and what you have yet to do. You have all the potentials within to enlighten yourself. If you understand and systematically practice all the steps, you will definitely progress.

Patanjali has divided the science of ashtanga yoga into two parts, external and internal. Yoga acknowledges that there are conflicts within and without. If you want to understand life, you have to make conscious effort to learn how to deal with all these conflicts. By practicing the first five steps that constitute the outer face of ashtanga yoga — *yama, niyama, asana, pranayama* and *pratyahara* — you will gain the skill to deal with disturbances that come from the external world and to have control over your external activities. However, life is not limited to the external world or to exploration of the external world. You also have to take steps to understand and deal with internal disturbances, which are deeper and stronger. In the ladder of ashtanga yoga the last three steps are internal: *dharana, dhyana* and *samadhi*. These three steps comprise internal techniques that lead to control over mind and its modifications, or perfect self-control.

You are aware of your conscious mind and senses, that part of mind you have been educating to be successful in the world and to enjoy life, but you do not realize that the conscious mind is merely a small part of the totality of the mind. If you come to comprehend the entire mind and all its functions, you will realize that the real source of disturbances is your mind. When you become aware of the totality of the mind, you can easily gain control of that part of mind you use during the waking state. You can even learn to control the dreaming mind that functions only during the dreaming state. Likewise the part of mind that creates a state of deep sleep for you can be brought under conscious control. Then only can you attain the fourth state, turiya, the superconscious state of your mind.

The first two rungs of the ladder of ashtanga yoga consist of ten moral commitments, the *yamas* (restraints) and the *niyamas* (observances). The persistent practice of the yamas and niyamas is the foundation of yoga sadhana. If you practice these ten commitments, you will comprehend the basic principles of yoga sadhana and all the great religions of the world.

To Be **COMMITTED** to Something Means to Do It with **FULL** Dedication and Sincerity

These commitments are not vows that you take or that someone imposes on you. If you take vows and then you do something against those vows, you will suffer from a guilt complex. On the other hand, if you are fully committed to doing something, it means you are doing it because you want to do it, you have a clear understanding of what you are doing and you consider it to be good for your growth. To be committed to something means to do it with full dedication and sincerity. Don't be puffed up with pride or go on an ego trip; understand that you are committing yourself in order to improve yourself. Don't undertake a spiritual practice unless you are very sure. Otherwise you will be wasting your time and energy. The first thing to do is to build your sankalpa shakti: *I will do it. I can do it, I have to do it and I am fully equipped to do it.* Understand the technique fully, and then practise it. If the technique is perfect, and you practise it according to the way described, you will get results. If not, either there is something wrong with the technique, or you have not properly prepared your mind.

There are two sets of commitments because you are citizens of two worlds — the world within and the external

world. The first set of commitments, the yamas, is meant
to improve your relationships in the external world. The
second set, the niyamas, helps you improve yourself
from within. Even though you may be very peaceful
within, you may not know how to maintain peace in your
relationships. You have to create a bridge between the two
worlds. While the yamas apply to society, the niyamas
pertain to the individual.

The *yamas* are five restraints that help you to regulate
your relationships with other beings. They are: *ahimsa,*
how to express love in the external world by not causing
pain to anyone by thought, word or deed; *satya,* how to
practise truth by thinking, speaking and acting the truth;
asteya, how to remain a person of strength from within
by not taking or coveting what belongs to others in the
form of theft, fornication, plagiarism, embezzlement,
breach of trust, deception, cheating or exploitation of the
ignorant and the unwary; *brahmacharya,* how to conserve
and utilize your energy; and *aparigraha,* abandoning
nonessential articles of dress, food, furniture and other
paraphernalia of worldly life, and not expecting anything
from others. These ten commitments are not conditioned
by class, place, time or occasion and extend to all stages of
your practice.

Ahimsa

Ahimsa is the first commitment. In Sanskrit *a* prefixed
to a word means "not" and *himsa* means "harming, injuring,
hurting, or killing." Thus *ahimsa* means "nonhurting
or nonviolence in thought, speech and action." Ahimsa
is a negative virtue. Patanjali is not telling you to do
something; he is speaking from a different viewpoint and

instructing you not to do that which is not to be done. You don't have to worry about having to do good deeds. By not harming anyone you will be doing what is right.

First apply ahimsa to yourself by not hurting yourself in thought, speech or action. On the path of enlightenment one of the first things you have to learn is not to condemn yourself. You have formed the bad habit of identifying with your thought patterns, and so your thinking process controls your whole life. When you identify with your thoughts either you think you are bad or else you become puffed up with pride, neither of which is helpful. One cripples your creative intelligence and the other feeds the ego. A thought cannot make you good or bad. If a negative thought passes through your mind, it does not mean you are bad. It is your choice to accept or reject any thought that comes. There is no need to condemn yourself or feel guilty. The important thing is to be able to recognize which thoughts are helpful and which are to be rejected. For this you will have to sharpen the buddhi, the decisive faculty. If a thought is bad, let the thought be bad. It does not mean you are bad, because you are not your thoughts. You are much more than your thoughts. When you become aware that the powerful, merciful Lord who is omnipresent and omniscient is within you also, you will no longer condemn yourself.

Next you can initiate the practice of ahimsa at home. The family is a training center for learning how to love others. If you fail to love your family, you will also fail in other relationships. Husband and wife and other family members should never hurt each other. If married persons were to truly practise ahimsa, they would never quarrel. You should have an understanding in your relationships that no matter what happens you will not become violent. The practical approach to ahimsa is to practise nonviolence in thought, speech and action. It is not okay to love some people and hate others. The power of hatred definitely has a deeper impact on you than the power of love, because your love is too shallow. When you hate someone, you think of that person all the time. But the person you hate is not suffering; you are suffering, because they are your thoughts.

When animosity controls your mind, it leads your mind toward negativity. It is the defense mechanism that creates many of the problems you have in communication. If you are afraid of me and I am afraid of you, there can be no communication between us. We both become defensive and then we fight. This is what happens between two nations, and that is why the whole world is fighting. We are all human beings and there is only one source that is supplying the life force to everyone. There is only one proprietor of all persons and things, and everyone is breathing the same air, no matter which community, religion or culture one comes from. Therefore you have no right to hate or harm anyone. We are all the children of one eternity. Confusion arises when you forget there is only one absolute power that is all pervading. Once you realize this, it will not be possible for you to hate or hurt others.

Violence in speech or in action is almost always preceded by violent thoughts, which have serious repercussions on the mind and body. When you hurt someone or you think about somebody negatively, not only are you wasting time and energy, you are hurting yourself. When you hate others, it is you who suffers, not the rest of the world. Thought power is very important. All negativity can be washed away and the mind can be purified if you learn to forgive others. You also have many weaknesses and perhaps you are projecting those weaknesses onto others. Negative thoughts, emotions and violent behavior come when your reason is not functioning. Never allow your reason to retire or waste your energy in violence and negativity. Violence and anger diminish the power of love and gentleness. It is important to make effort to redirect negativity toward positive thinking. Patanjali says constant contemplation on the opposite is the way to get freedom from hatred and violence. For example, if somebody hates you or if you have negative feelings toward someone, try to think of that person in a loving way. Your love should travel toward expansion, not contraction. If you can learn to love your enemies, they will no longer be enemies to you. Love is more powerful than animosity.

The true expression of love is noninjuring, nonhurting, nonharming and nonkilling in daily life. You will never know what love is if you do not understand these four things. You cannot hurt someone and at the same time say I love you. Learn to love others and demonstrate that love through selfless action. To love someone does not mean to be attached. Love means to give selflessly; attachment means to possess. When you possess something, you are expanding the domain of your ego; when you love, you are surrendering your ego.

In the practice of ahimsa, give the best that you can selflessly to those whom you love and those who claim to love you, without any condition or expectation. If you expect something in return, then the quality of your love will be reduced by fifty per cent. You will experience great joy when you do something for others without expectation of any return. The law is: *Give and you will receive.* If you want to love and serve others without any selfish motivation or desire for reward, you will have to make effort to observe your thoughts, action and speech. Throughout human history and civilization there have been countless individuals who have made the pilgrimage from a narrow focus on *I, me* and *mine* to the much more broadened viewpoint of choosing to love and serve the higher good of society. And as they increasingly dedicated themselves to the benefit of humankind and the recognition of the universal consciousness in all, numerous powers unfolded in them. Those great individuals like Christ, Buddha, Gandhi and others all saw themselves as instruments of a higher force of consciousness, love and power in the universe, not as petty human beings preoccupied with trivial desires and pleasures. They were perfect embodiments of love and universal examples of the true expression of ahimsa.

Patanjali says, *ahimsa pratishthayam tat samniddhau vairatyagah* (When one is firmly established in ahimsa, others let go of any hostility in that person's presence). If you sincerely follow ahimsa with mind, action and speech, even the most ferocious animal will become calm and quiet in your presence. Many yogis practising in the deep forests of the jungle have experienced this phenomenon. When you have no desire or thought to kill any animal, why should an animal want to kill you? If you are truly established in ahimsa, you will radiate love and no one will hurt you. Animals, even the deadliest of snakes and the most vicious animals, will transform into loving creatures before you. If you are not afraid, you will not invite danger. I can give you one example from my own experience:

When I was just eleven years of age, Rishikesh was very different than it is today. At that time it was not polluted or crowded and it was mostly forests. One day after taking a dip in the Ganges, my master took me to the nearby Virbhadra temple to meditate. I was still a child, so naturally I kept opening and closing my eyes after every few minutes. Once when I opened my eyes I was horrified to see a cobra sitting just one meter away from me! My Lord, I became so afraid! I closed my eyes again and tried to meditate, but I could only meditate on the cobra. I dared to open my eyes only a slit and every time I did so I saw that the cobra was still calmly sitting there. I decided I would get up as soon as the cobra went away. The whole time I was supposed to be meditating I actually was thinking about and meditating on that cobra. After some time I was so frightened I could wait no longer and I started to get up to run away. Sensing my restlessness my master asked, "What is the matter with you?"

"A cobra is sitting next to me and you ask what's the matter with me? Do you want me to die?"

Without losing his composure he replied, "When you are in a meditative state, even animals around you will remain calm because meditation is very powerful. There is no need to run away."

A few minutes later the cobra quietly slithered away. Then my master told me I would have

an ashram at that site after thirty-five years.
I completely forgot about that incident until
thirty-five years later when I started to build
my ashram at Rishikesh.

To practise the philosophy of loving all and
excluding none in daily life is to practise nonviolence.
There can be no hostility in the presence of a yogi who is
firmly established in the practice of nonviolence. Only a
person who is very strong can practise true nonviolence,
such as the Buddha:

There was one robber who used to cut off the
fingers of those whom he robbed. Somebody had
told him that if he would cut off one thousand
and one fingers of living human beings he
would become a great and enlightened being.
Throughout the years he had collected many
fingers but still he needed a few more. Since he
was having difficulty finding anyone else, in
his impatience he decided he would cut off his
mother's fingers. When she came to know what
he planned to do she tried to run away, but he
chased her. By chance, Buddha was walking
and saw them running on the other side of the
road. When he realized what was happening,
he quickly crossed the road and pushed her
behind him to protect her. Holding his hands
out to the robber, he said, "Here are the fingers
you need."

When the robber raised his sword to cut Buddha's fingers he was stunned that it would not come down, no matter how hard he tried. This was because Buddha practised perfect ahimsa.

The greatest of all strengths comes from within and that is the strength of love. A gentle, loving person is very strong from within; such a person knows how to love and also how to protect himself. Self-defense is not an act of violence. In my childhood my master sent me to learn kung fu because he saw that I was becoming very weak. Now I can defend myself against four or five people at the same time. Before they could even think about hurting me, they would be on the ground.

When you learn to make your mind inward and one-pointed you fathom those boundaries you have created for yourself and you come to understand that deep within you is the source, the Self of all. There you will find the all-encompassing love that emanates through your mind, action and speech. Strength lies in love not in violence. Violence comes from weakness. You can learn to be strong by cultivating constant awareness that you are Atman. The Atman within you, not the body, breath, mind or your individuality, is the same as Paramatman.

So the first thing Patanjali teaches is to be sensitive toward others and what they are feeling, to love all and exclude none. You lose sensitivity when you become selfish and egotistical. You close yourself off to others and cut yourself off from your surroundings. You remain in that shell thinking you know everything, you have everything and you are happy. You all aspire for love but you do not know what it is, because nobody has taught you how to love. During the waking state, you worry and talk about this love and that love. But what happens to your love when you go to sleep or when you dream? Your so-called human love is subject to your conscious mind alone. You are not aware of that love when you sleep. However the life force is present whether you are awake, dreaming or sleeping, because it is the real center of your love.

Careful cultivation of ahimsa will lead to spontaneous, all-encompassing love. The practice of ahimsa encompasses the principles of how to love yourself and others, and how to have that sensitivity that inspires you to serve others without expecting any reward or having any selfish motivation. Selflessness is an expression of love and can lead you to right spirituality. Eventually, the day will come when you will start to love everyone, for beneath all these forms and names there is only one reality. Through the practice of ahimsa, you can learn to love all. Then you will radiate love and your mind will remain in a state of joy. That is one of the greatest qualities you can develop. It can happen when your consciousness awakens and travels to higher dimensions.

Love for a human being is entirely different than love for God. When two people love the same girl, they may become so blinded by rage and jealousy they could even kill each other. But when two people love God, they will also love each other. Love for God is universal; the other love is personal. Personal love is also valid because it teaches you how to truly love and expand yourself to universal consciousness. That which brings transformation is love. Love is perfect knowledge. But if you do not have a major transfusion of human compassion, you can never have divine love.

Satya

First is love, and then comes *satya* (truth). If you want to practise and know truth, first you should practise ahimsa: *satyam bruyat priyam bruyat* (Speak the truth, say what is loving and pleasant).

A great sage once beautifully explained satya: "To know truth you have to practise truthfulness with mind, action and speech. And if you have known truth with mind, action and speech, you have known everything. There is nothing more to know than that."

It will be difficult for you to practise truth if you do not know how to express and communicate love. You should speak only truth that is inseparably mingled with love. Truth that is harsh or hurtful is not needed. Suppose I see a blind man coming and I say, "Hey, you blind man. Come over here." That is *apriya* (hurtful or unloving). I am not lying, but that truth is crude and hurtful. Truth that hurts is not satya. Speak the truth, but that truth should be pleasant, not the bitter truth. Don't speak what is not to be spoken or try to become a great teacher of truth by hurting people.

In the context of this aphorism truth does not refer to the abstract or philosophical truth, or as the scriptures say, the ultimate truth, or God. Absolute truth is absolute truth. Patanjali is not saying to practise that truth. There is no need to run to a church, a temple or a swami when you think of truth. You are not practising satya when you say, "God is truth, and truth is God." Patanjali is talking about the principle truth that you use and practise in daily life. To practise truth means to speak what you know to be fact, to act in a way that you understand to be correct and to train your mind to follow a train of thought that is helpful for you. Satya means to be truthful to yourself and to others in thought, speech and action.

We all learned the same principles in childhood: *Be kind, be gentle and strong; be loving and truthful.* We know the principles, but no one taught us how to practise them. That is why the human personality is full of conflicts. Everyone says to speak the truth, yet no one provides an example of how to be truthful. You know what a lie is, but you do not yet know what truth is. Truth is the principle, but practice is different from principle.

To begin with, observe how much you talk and try to talk less. Those who talk a lot tend to speak nonsense and waste a lot of time and energy. That is why yoga advocates the practice of silence. If you have the habit of talking all the time, you will find it very difficult to remain in silence.

Next, decide that no matter what happens, you will not say anything that is not based on fact. Patanjali does not say to be truthful. He says by not lying you are practising truthfulness. Just as with ahimsa, Patanjali is telling you not to do what is not to be done. This is *nishedha*. The opposite of nishedha is *vidhi*, that which should be done. To practise satya you should apply the first principle, nishedha. The strongest word in the world is no. In Sanskrit and Hindi it is *na. Na karo. Don't do it. Do you want to do it? Na.* Finished. *Do you want to eat? Na.* How powerful it is. Patanjali is making you aware that the negative can be used positively. By not doing what should not be done, you are doing what should be done. You practise ahimsa by not hurting anyone and satya by not lying. There is no need to boast that you are speaking truth. My master taught me not to tell others to speak truth nor to claim that I was speaking truth. In my childhood the swamis in the cave monastery would spank me if I lied. They kept telling me to speak the truth:

Before I left the monastery to attend college the sadhu who was keeping accounts said to me, "You are the greatest liar in this tradition! Although you are in the tradition, you have not yet joined the tradition as a teacher. You have lied consciously 156 times."

I said, "No, now you are lying! Tell me, when did I lie?"

He began, "On such and such day you said this," and he proceeded to give a detailed and complete record of all my lies that he had recorded in his memory.

I responded, "It is very difficult to even think in front of you big guys, you know. If I just think something, you come out and ask me, 'Why are you thinking this way?'"

Actually I never took these things as criticism because they helped me a lot. To live in the company of sages is a great privilege. Tagore has written, "In this poisonous tree of life, there are two immortal fruits. One is awareness of the eternal, and the other is the company of the sages. If you are in such company, you should be grateful to the Lord."

One day I said to my master, "I know that I should speak the truth, but I don't know how. Tell me, what is that truth?"

He answered, "The simplest way to speak truth is by not lying. If you do not lie, you are speaking truth. But if you say you are speaking truth, and you do not know what truth is, that is confusion, not truth. Simply do not lie. Do not do what is not to be done according to your conscience and you will be doing what is right."

Yoga science says you are constantly blasting and hurting your inner being by lying. Even though you know you are lying, still you continue to do so. Every time you lie, you are creating a serious division between your heart and mind. You are hurting yourself, not others. According to your capacity, try not to lie. The first step is not to make up something that is not true. If I ask you something and you don't know the answer, simply say you don't know instead of making up something. If you don't want to say anything, you can remain quiet, as long as you are being truthful. Don't be dishonest. If you frequently lie, it becomes an unconscious habit that affects your personality and creates obstacles to your growth. Sometimes you lie because you are afraid of what will happen if you tell the truth. One lie leads to another, and soon deception becomes second nature, leading to a fearful and scheming mind. To avoid this, always stick to the facts. Be straight and gentle when you speak and then your speech will be effective. If you do not lie and your actions are truthful, you will stand as an example to others.

It is not so easy to avoid telling lies. Once you determine that you will not lie, you will find many obstacles in the way, just waiting to convince you to lie! Someone will try to persuade you it is better to lie. Another will offer love to you to lie. If you resist that, then somebody else may even try to force you or threaten you. But if you have known the gentle strength of the truth within, and if you stand on that, you will become victorious, just as the stationmaster in the following story:

I used to travel by rail with my master when we had to go long distances. I remember sitting with him at a railroad station when I was just sixteen years of age, which is a very irresponsible age. We all have gone through that. The stationmaster walked over to me and said, "Sir, please give me something to practise. I promise that I will regularly practise it."

Before I could respond, my master told me
to teach him something. I politely declined,
"But I myself am a fool. Why should one fool
misguide another fool? I think it is better if you
teach him."

So he told the stationmaster, "I will agree to
teach you only if you promise that you are
definitely going to practise what I teach you."

The stationmaster agreed, so my master gave
him the following practice: "From today on,
don't lie. That's all. And if you faithfully follow
this practice for three months and you are not
enlightened, I will leave this world. That is my
promise to you. I'm not telling you to speak the
truth, because that would be very difficult to
do. Just don't lie."

The stationmaster again vowed to keep his
promise to my master. He did not know it at
the time, but his troubles were just beginning.
He was soon to be fired from his job. It was
common knowledge that everyone at the
station was taking bribes. When the inspector
came and began to question the stationmaster
about the other employees, this time he
could not lie to him. As a result they were all
prosecuted and the stationmaster was fired,
because now everyone was against him.

And the man thought, *O Lord! It has only been
thirteen days! What is going to happen to me in
three months' time?*

Everything bad that could happen, happened
to him: his wife and children left him in one
month's time, and his whole life fell apart.

One afternoon my master was lying under a tree on the bank of the Narmada River and he was smiling. I asked him why he was smiling. He replied, "It is very difficult to practise the truth, but it is more difficult not to lie."

Defensively I said, "But I don't lie to you!"

Whatever he asked me, I answered him truthfully. There was no need to lie to him because I was not afraid of him. I was very frank with him about whatever I did. Sometimes I was so frank, he would close my mouth and tell me to shut up: "What are you talking about? This is no way for you to talk to your master."

Then he brought up the stationmaster again. "Do you know what is happening to that stationmaster? That man that I told not to lie is now in jail."

"So why are you laughing?"

"I'm not laughing at him or at myself; I'm laughing at the foolish world. The twelve people who worked in his office habitually took bribes, so in order to save themselves they formed a group and conspired against him. They claimed he was lying, even though he was speaking the truth. In the courtroom the stationmaster said to the judge, "Sir, no matter how many years you put me behind bars, I won't lie. For me, you are a symbol of truth, and I will never lie to you."

The judge looked at him and asked, "Where is your attorney? I think you need somebody to help you."

"I don't need a lawyer. I cannot lie, so why do I need an attorney? I also used to take bribes and share them with the other people in the office, but then I met a swami who told me not to lie no matter what happens. Since then, in only one month's time, I have lost my job, my wife and children have left me, I have no money and I am about to be put behind bars. And he told me not to lie for three months! No matter what happens, Sir, please just put me behind bars. I don't care."

The judge did not know what to do so he said, "Okay, we will recess for one hour and then continue."

Then he quietly called the prosecuting attorney to accompany him and the stationmaster to his chamber. He said to the stationmaster, "Tell me who your master is."

Fortunately for the stationmaster it turned out that the judge was also a disciple of my master. So he acquitted him and said, "You are on the right path, no matter what happens. I wish I could be with you!"

And so, when the man was released after three months, he had nothing left. He was sitting under a tree by the side of a street when someone came and delivered a telegram to him that said:

Your father had a large piece of land that was taken by the government, and now the government wants to give you some compensation.

That compensation came to two million rupees! He had not known about the land, because it was in a different province. He realized he had completed the three months' commitment that day. "Not lying has rewarded me so much!" he exclaimed.

He gave one million rupees to his wife and children. They were very happy and asked him to come home. But he refused and said, "No, not anymore. So far, I have only seen what happens by not lying. Now, I'm going to see what happens by knowing truth."

So first you should learn nishedha and eliminate what is not truth. You can transform your personality completely provided you are practical, truthful and sincere to yourself. Don't be concerned with what others say about you. The world gives you many suggestions the whole day, from morning till evening. Don't be afraid or controlled by those suggestions. For example, suppose your husband keeps telling you that you are not a good person. Even though you know he has no right to judge you, if you are weak, you accept and believe his suggestions. You may even start to behave accordingly. At other times he may tell you how beautiful you are. This confuses you and you don't know what to believe. You have to be strong to go through the procession of life, because you are blasted by suggestions from all quarters. If you go on thinking you are bad, you will definitely become bad. If on the other hand you repeat to yourself that you are good, you will feel more positive about yourself. Both self-suggestions and suggestions from others can have a deep effect. You have allowed yourself to be so influenced by society and other people's suggestions that you have lost your individuality and you rarely act according to your own thinking. Sometimes you may want to speak truth but you cannot because others don't allow it. This happened to me when I started to do experiments in the United States to demonstrate the power of yoga. Initially the scientists and religionists were very happy with the experiments. But when they could not understand what I was doing or how it was possible for me to do such things, they decided that what I was doing was against their religious beliefs. Then they started to verbally attack me and tried to undo what I had done. Such human prejudices hamper the progress of humanity.

We all talk about truth and about speaking the truth, but nobody likes to hear the truth. When you are not prepared to hear the truth about yourself, how can you think you are prepared to know the omnipresent and omniscient truth?

To be truthful to yourself you only need to rely on your conscience, the mirror within. You have not yet realized the reality that is deep within you because you have the habit of seeing things externally rather than going to the heart of the matter. To look within you have to follow an inward process. You think you need a teacher to help and guide you in the inward method because you have formed a bad habit of depending on something external all the time. But you don't need anyone to teach you the inward process. There is something within you that is neither your mind nor intellect that will always guide you and tell you the truth, and wants you to be enlightened. That is your conscience. The conscience is not the mind; through the mind you can only intellectualize things. Your conscience is a mirror within that cannot be separated from your whole being. You can ask your conscience anytime how you are doing and it will truthfully respond. Even if you are not the best person, you can be certain that your conscience will never lie to you. One of the first and most essential steps of the path of enlightenment is to learn to consult and follow the guidance of your conscience.

The conscience is that part of your life that keeps an account of your deeds, externally and internally. It is at your disposal all the time and, if you are willing to listen to it, will tell you what you are doing wrong. There is no need to ask anyone else. But you don't want to know that part of yourself or to have a real encounter with life. You don't want to consult your conscience, because your habits are stronger than your conscience. You keep trying to escape from your own reality by going to the movies or telephoning a friend when you feel sad. You have developed a habit of escapism and it has become a very strong part of your life. Now you have to develop the habit of consulting your conscience when you are in need of guidance. Sometimes when you feel lost you may sit down and pray to ask God for guidance. You have to be realistic. You know God will not come to you and directly give you guidance. But if you look within and ask your conscience for guidance, it will immediately respond to you. There is no need to depend on anything external. No matter how bad you are, whether you are a thief, a liar or whatever, your conscience will tell you what to do next. Once, when I lived with one of the sages, I had an interesting experience:

As far as I knew, there was no one else in the room besides the two of us, but I could hear the sage talking with someone throughout the night. I was very curious and so in the morning I asked him, "Swamiji, why didn't you introduce me to your visitor last night?"

"There was no one with me, I assure you."

I decided to be more direct and asked, "Then with whom were you talking?"

"I was talking to myself."

I said, "In the western world, if you talk to yourself, people will call you insane."

He patiently replied, "This is not insanity. You can talk to yourself, to your conscience, when no one is listening. If you develop this habit, you will find that deep down within you there is one who answers very honestly, even though you are not honest with that part of yourself. This is called self-dialogue."

In many of the teachings of the great scriptures there is a dialogue between one who is perfect and one who is striving to be perfect. Similarly, when you have an internal dialogue, the conversation is between the imperfect part of you that asks the questions and your conscience that replies truthfully. Once you become aware of your conscience and regularly consult it, you can direct the course of your whole life.

Your gestures and behavior often contradict your inner feelings. For example you may not really feel like smiling, yet you smile. Instead of being honest, you smile and pretend to be happy, even though you are miserable and feel that you are wasting your life. This misery of phoniness makes you feel more and more despondent. Be practical. Train yourself not to be affected by the external world. Be a perfect actor in the world and consciously distance your mind from your external activities so the world does not affect you inside. Learn to express what you feel, no matter what happens. Then there will be no difference between what you are within or without.

You have been listening to everyone else throughout your life. Now decide to seek advice only from your conscience. Do an experiment for one week and listen to your conscience, not your ego. During that time don't consult anyone else or depend on anyone external. Stop living your life according to the opinions of others. Instead, sit down quietly, and analyze what is wrong with your actions or speech. Consider what you have been doing, decide what has not been helpful for you and then simply don't repeat it. You can easily do this. Work with yourself slowly and gently. Your conscience will tell you the truth. The whole world may tell you that you are a great man, but your conscience will tell you otherwise. You will see yourself as you really are in the mirror of your conscience. In addition, when you counsel within, you will discover the vastness of internal life as compared with the external world. You can know all the levels of your life if you go within, but if you keep roaming around in the external world, you will only become a travel addict. You will not gain anything lasting by going from one country to another. The day you start to consult your conscience is the first step in the path of enlightenment.

When you rely on your conscience for guidance, you will become very gentle, yet very strong, so that the world will have no power to disturb you. If you want to examine your strength, observe how many times in a day you become disturbed by what others say or do. Only a weak person is easily disturbed. I am not talking of physical strength, but of that strength that comes from within. Authority and responsibilities do not make anyone strong. What can make you strong is the gentleness that comes from a source of inner strength.

You may think you know what truth is but even if you read all the bibles of the world and listen to many sages and swamis, you will not know truth unless you practise it. You can write or say the word *God*, but this does not mean you know what God is. Similarly, merely saying or writing the word *truth* cannot teach you what truth means. To know truth, learn to speak truth by not lying. To understand truth it is not necessary to follow any particular religion. You simply have to be a student of life. In the relative world there are two forces: one is right, satya, and the other is wrong, *mithya* (falsehood).

Truth has great power. The day you really know how to speak truth, your words will have great weight. Only those who are selfless can practise true satya. It is said that if a person makes truth the central focus of his life, all of his utterances will come true, for such a person is incapable of speaking something that is not true. The ultimate result of being fully established in truthfulness is that all kinds of gems and the best things of the world present themselves before such a person because he deserves them, though he does not need them.

When you are truly honest, you will receive the power of clairvoyance. This means you will see everything very clearly, even those things that are hidden to the human mind and eye in normal conditions, and you will no longer experience confusion or cloudiness:

Once a swami explained the meaning of clairvoyance to me and I said, "That is not possible. Nobody can do that."

So he gave me a practical demonstration and then he said, "Now you have to do it."

"I will, but first you must teach me how to practise."

I practised according to his instructions and found that what he told me was absolutely true.

If you have a burning desire within, and you work with yourself a few minutes everyday, you also can become clairvoyant. Clairvoyance is not something weird or fake. It means to have the capacity to see things clearly and to easily penetrate into the deeper levels of your being.

Asteya

Asteya, the third commitment, means "nonstealing." Stealing is another habit that weakens you and cripples your personality. The legal definition of theft is: *To take what belongs to someone else without that person's permission.*

When you steal you are depriving someone of what is rightfully his. Self-awareness is always with us, but real awareness means to become aware that others also exist. As you respect your own existence, you have to respect the existence of others. All human beings have the same rights and you have no right to deprive anyone else of those rights.

Even if you are successful in stealing, you are hurting yourself. It is a bad habit to steal because it weakens your willpower and conscience, and dissipates and distracts the mind. If you are truly honest you will never be attracted to another person's possessions or wealth. Only a weak person can steal. To overcome this weakness you have to try to strengthen your willpower throughout your whole life. My master taught me from a very early age not to steal:

Once when I was five years of age, I put my hand into my master's pocket and took out five rupees and did not tell him. He immediately knew what I had done and scolded me, "You have stolen something."

I denied it and told him I had not stolen his rupees.

"You have taken them without my permission and that is theft. If you tell me that you are taking something, it is not theft."

I understood the difference.

No matter how much you are tempted, don't form the habit of stealing. If you have many things and someone steals all those things, even if you have nothing, still you are richer than the person who has stolen from you.

When you do something good, it comes from your conscience. When you feel bad about yourself, you condemn yourself or you are weak, it is your mind that is responsible. Suppose you have a habit of doing something your conscience doesn't approve of such as stealing. You can learn to control that. Sit down and have a dialogue with your mind: *Okay mind, if you want to steal, go ahead, but I am not going to move my body; I am not going with you.* Then mind is helpless. You are not telling the mind to do anything and you are not going against your mind; you are simply controlling your body and not allowing your legs to take you to the place where you can steal the desired object. This is how to train your mind. If you repeat this every time mind wants to steal something, after some time you will find that mind will no longer be tempted, and your bad habit will be gone. When your mind realizes you are not going to do everything it dictates, then it will gradually come under your control. One who is conscientious will never steal. One who practises yoga knows it is harmful to steal because it weakens the willpower and distracts the mind.

Brahmacharya

Once you have practised how to love selflessly, how to practise truth relating with the facts, and how not to steal, then comes the fourth commitment, *brahmacharya*, or walking in Brahman consciousness. Brahman is the Absolute, the proprietor of all, who gives the breath of life to all of us. When you are conscious of the reality, you remain in Brahman consciousness. This is the highest meaning of brahmacharya. One who is conscious of the reality all the time is called a *brahmachari*.

There are so many deep meanings and connotations of the word *brahmacharya*, they could fill a huge volume that would be of great use to the world. Once I found an unpublished scripture on brahmacharya in the archives of the library of Ram Nagar, a city in the district of Varanasi. A brahmachari whose name was Dev Swami had written that scripture. He had no tongue by birth, but he became a great swami. It took me six months to study that scripture.

Literally, the word *brahmacharya* means "celibacy," but not only in the physical sense. Brahman is the omnipresent, omniscient and omnipotent Shakti, or the ultimate power; *charya* means "how to utilize that power." One who knows how to utilize the power of Shakti is called brahmachari. For a monk who has taken vows and wants to use his energy totally towards the goal of knowing God, a life of celibacy is appropriate. But worldly people can also practise brahmacharya by learning how to channel their energy in one direction. A brahmachari is one who knows how to conduct his energy in thought, speech and action and does not waste energy. For those who are renunciates it is essential to remain celibate. But for everyone else brahmacharya means to direct one's energy for a right use.

Brahmacharya is not limited to the sexual act. In married life, or *grihastha*, wife and husband are practicing brahmacharya when they do not allow their minds to be distracted here and there. If you are faithful to your wife, and she is faithful to you, you are both brahmacharis. In married life, your love should not be limited to the level of physical awareness and consciousness. It should expand to Atman. You are like two dots connected by marriage. If you draw a line of harmony between the two, two become one. This also is brahmacharya.

According to society the best way to deal with the biological necessity of sex is to get married. However most marital problems result from misunderstandings in the sexual relationship, due to lack of training. Insecurity in the sexual relationship is one of the major causes of divorce all over the world. Many of the couples I have counseled have fallen apart because of this issue. A woman's constitution is entirely different from a man's. Without any consideration a man sometimes acts like a brute force. He rushes from outside, performs the sexual act and then goes away. He doesn't understand the repercussions such behavior could have on a woman. Love should come first and sex should follow, because sex originates in the mind and then goes through the body. When you eat food, the body is satisfied first, and the mind afterward. There is a vast difference.

If you suddenly abstain from sex, you may start to have nightmares or feel the need to masturbate frequently. Or maybe you are sexually active but still your mind remains preoccupied with sex all the time. Patanjali is not telling you to do sex or not to do it. But if you force yourself to abstain from sex, it will become a great obstacle in the path. It is up to you to decide. It is possible to live without sex and a home and family. It all depends on what you want to do. *Brahmacharya* means to first understand all your levels of energy and what your capacity is, and not to direct all your energy toward sex alone. Those who have control over their energy, have the power to do sex as enjoyment. The rest may want to enjoy but are not successful.

The monastic way of life is very different from life in the world. Two advanced practices are taught in our cave monastery: how to die consciously and come back; and *urdhva-retas* (literally, upward-traveling semen; the practice of leading the semen upward). *Urdhva* means "upward traveling," *retas* is "semen." There was a time when total abstinence from sex was absolute law for the students in the cave monasteries. However, since nobody was able to faithfully follow this law, students were taught the ancient technique of urdhva-retas. Initiation into this practice was first introduced in the Vedic period, some five thousand years ago, and this tradition has continued unbroken since then. The student is given the first initiation into this practice after twelve to fourteen years of apprenticeship. That initiation helps them to experience enjoyment that is higher than the joy of sexual union.

The student first learns how to concentrate on particular energy fields to stimulate the sex glands to produce semen. Then by the use of mental power he creates enough heat to evaporate the seminal secretions. This subtle vapor then rises upward through the centralis canalis of the spinal cord to the brain, after which it is again circulated, so that nothing is wasted.

There are a few misconceptions regarding this practice that I would like to rectify. One who practises urdhva-retas does not become impotent. He can still get married and have children if he wants. Rather it is a powerful practice that helps to develop complete control over ejaculation. With such control the student will no longer have nightmares or dream about sex; he won't feel the need to run around chasing women like a stupid fellow. Whatever he does, he will do it with conscious control. The purpose of the practice of urdhva-retas is to learn how to completely utilize the flow of energy rather than wasting it.

Another misconception is that only men can practise urdhva-retas. This is not true. Both women and men can practise it, but initiation is given only to students in the monasteries. This practice is not known to the world. The world knows only one way — to discharge semen and call it sex and enjoyment. That joy is nothing compared with the joy of urdhva-retas. You cannot imagine how much enjoyment you would have if you knew the technique of how to retain the sexual energy. For one who knows how to control sexual energy, retention gives a far greater joy, whereas sexual union gives only a glimpse of that joy. You keep searching for a way to expand the joy of sexual union and make it last forever, but you are searching at the wrong place, like churning sand for oil. Physical union cannot lead to permanent, perfect and everlasting bliss, *ananda*. There are two types of ananda. One is *vishayananda* and the other is *paramananda:* momentary bliss and perennial bliss. The sexual act is vishayananda, a mere glimpse of joy. You keep doing it again and again with the hope that it will become perennial joy. But you can experience paramananda only when you go to a higher level of consciousness. My master told me that the whole world thinks that sexual union is the greatest joy. He added, "I don't agree. But if you take out the word *sexual* and just say union is the greatest joy, then I will agree."

There are other techniques besides sexual abstinence that brahmacharis use to develop tremendous physical

strength. Some of these techniques have been externalized
in ritual worship in the Hindu religion and the real
meaning and purpose and the correct way to practise
them have been forgotten. For example, the following is a
spiritual *yantra* (symbol):

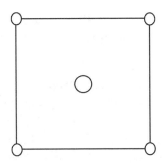

Those who are familiar with Hindu Shiva temples will
recognize the structure. There are four corners of the
temple and in the center is the *lingam*, a symbol of Lord
Shiva. Nowadays people pour water over the lingam and
worship it, or a pot with a small hole in the bottom is
placed above the lingam, so water can continuously drip
onto the lingam. The water is symbolic of the nectar that
drips onto the internal lingam, *"Loob dub, loob dub,"* like
the sound of the beating of the heart that is heard through
a stethoscope. Devotees don't understand that what they
are doing is in reality an external representation of a
yogic practice, and the correct way to practise it has been
forgotten.

Actually you are a temple yourself, so it is not
necessary to go to any external temple to perform thsese
practices. Of all these practices, khechari mudra is said to
be supreme. By the practice of khechari mudra one gains

three things: control over *vishuddha* chakra; control over *bindu* (seed of life, here vital force, prana); and control of the sexual urge, both the inner manifestation (*ojas*) and the outer manifestation (semen), so that even if one were embraced by a beautiful naked woman, he would not be influenced in the least. It is bindu that sustains the body with its network of *nadis* (energy channels) and nourishes all the gland centers. Any sensation of pleasure or enjoyment is an indication of the presence of bindu.

In this practice one drinks the nectar of the moon, also referred to as *soma*, which is secreted from a center in the head corresponding to the physical choroid plexus, from where the cerebrospinal fluid is secreted. It is this nectar that gives the body power, resistance and growth. If it is wasted or falls into the solar plexus where the sun (*agni* or *pitta*) dries it up, the body becomes ill and old age prematurely creeps in.

A yogi who consistently practises khechari mudra daily becomes pure, free from all diseases, grows beautiful in body and lives a very long and healthy life. He continually enjoys heavenly bliss and in the next incarnation is born in a great family. By perfecting the practice of khechari mudra in *shirshasana* (headstand) along with the application of *mulabandha* (root lock) and *uddiyana bandha* (abdominal lift) with pranayama, an old man is said to become rejuvenated and can decide when his death will take place; eventually he becomes immortal.

The technique is briefly described as follows: As with any advanced yogic practice, khechari mudra should only be practised under the guidance of a competent teacher. Each day, morning and evening, the tongue is milked with the fingers and pulled and stretched in all directions to make it supple and flexible. Before beginning, the tongue should be well lubricated with *ghee* (clarified butter). A tongue retractor can be used to allow you to grasp the tongue firmly without injuring it. Alternatively you can hold it with a silk cloth. The combined process of milking and sucking the tongue is to be kept up until the tip of the tongue can touch the space between the two eyebrows. Then it will be sufficiently elongated to enter the nasopharynx and close the three passageways: the larynx, pharynx and palate. After the milking and stretching, the tongue is turned back on itself and a sucking effort made to draw it back into the throat as far as possible in order to cover the orifice at the back of the nasal cavity and prevent air from escaping from the body. This is done during the *kumbhaka* (retention) stage of pranayama. You may repeat this exercise throughout the day whenever you think of it. In addition, once a week the frenulum or membrane beneath the tongue is cut one-sixteenth of an inch, or the thickness of a hair, and a little rock salt is put on the wound to prevent it from reuniting. This is continued until the full depth of this membrane is severed.

A modified form of khechari mudra is that of elongating the tongue so that it may be introduced into the nasal cavity, above the soft palate, to close the orifices of the two nostrils located in the skull. This is accomplished by the same process of milking and stretching it, anointing it, sucking and pushing the tongue to the back of the mouth. The turning of the tongue back upon itself may be aided with the fingers until it can enter this region on its own. At this point the tip of the tongue will correspond to the lower end of a line drawn vertically downwards from the pineal gland to the pituitary body; this line prolonged upward reaches the bregma, the point at which the coronal suture and sagittal sutures intersect. With the tongue in this position, the posterior border of the vomer can be distinctly felt in front. If the tip of the tongue is made to enter through each of the posterior nares the turgid mucous membrane of the obstructed side can be reached and it will feel hot and swollen like an onion. This turgidity will yield as the pressure is removed. On the side through which the air is passing freely, the mucous membrane does not feel so hot or swollen. The openings of the eustachian tubes and other anatomical details can also be easily felt. With persistent practice, the tongue can be made to actually touch ida, pingala and sushumna so that the flow through any one of these three nadis can be stopped at will.

There is no need to cut the frenulum for this modified form of khechari mudra. When the tongue can be extended so its tip touches the tip of the nose, it will be sufficiently elongated to attempt putting it over the soft palate. Then bend the handle of a teaspoon so as to make a hook and place this hook over the soft palate while applying gentle pressure downward and forward. Repeat this practice daily until all the soreness is gone and the membrane can be extended forward in the mouth. By pulling and stretching the soft palate for some days with the spoon, you will eventually find it possible to put the tongue behind the soft palate. At first you can use your fingers to position the tongue; before long you will easily be able to accomplish this unaided. If you slowly accommodate the sensitive nerves in that region to the touch of the tongue, all unpleasant sensations will disappear. Give at least six months to this practice. Never rush.

When you are successful at closing the two holes of the nostrils in the skull with the tongue while maintaining the suspension phase of respiration, the flow of vital fluid is restrained from leaving its place even during sexual intercourse. For one who is well advanced in the practice of khechari mudra, the nectar will flow from its place inside the head. This will counteract any and all poisons that may enter the body. This is brought about by the combination of kumbhaka and the heat generated while the tongue is fixed in this cavity. The point from which the nectar flows is situated on the left side of the space between the eyebrows. This is the source of the downward ida, pingala and sushumna nadis, and is known as the generator of knowledge when stimulated into action. This is also the place from which the physical body is shed at the time of death. When the fluid begins to drip, one experiences a number of known tastes such as salty, alkaline, bitter and astringent. These are followed by the feel and taste of ghee, then of milk, honey, palm juice and finally the taste of the nectar, or soma, which is a taste unlike any other essence. Actually the nectar has two different tastes: *svalpakala* and *amritakala*. Svalpakala makes you beautiful like Sarasvati, the goddess of wisdom; the other, amritakala, makes you very strong. Consequently those yogis who do this practice can be one of two types: One will be like Shankaracharya who tasted svalpakala and thus was very gentle and extraordinarily beautiful; the other will be like Dayananda, who tasted amritakala and was very strong physically. Like Dayananda, the power of a true brahmachari is immense:

Once in Jaipur, four horses and a buggy were stalled in the middle of the road. The horses were jumping and trying to go forward, but the buggy wouldn't move. Those who were sitting in the buggy could not understand what was happening. They turned around and were surprised to see that a swami was holding on to the back of the buggy, preventing it from moving. He asked them, "Do you only have four horses? Why don't you bring another ten horses!"

Someone asked him, "Sir, who are you?"

He answered, "I am a brahmachari. The difference between you and me is that you have lost your strength and I have not."

Some commentators on Patanjali's Yoga Sutras have used the word abstinence to translate the word *brahmacharya*. This is merely a superficial meaning. A more accurate translation is: *On being firmly established in sexual control, vigor is gained.* It's a very simple thing. One who does not do sex can become very powerful. *Brahman* means "Shakti," the power within you, and *charya* means "the way you utilize this power." This power is not limited to the sexual act, but you can examine your power by observing how much control you have in the sexual act. There are people who think about sex all the time and all of their energy is directed towards sex. When this happens it is considered to be a disease. Unfortunately modern society not only allows such an attitude toward sex, but also cultivates and encourages it.

The path of action in the world requires discipline on all levels. If you understand the four primitive fountains — food, sex, sleep and self-preservation — you will accept that it is important for you to discipline yourself. Discipline makes you aware of your capacity and of the resources and potentials that you have. Whether you overdo things or you do nothing you are hurting yourself. Neither extreme is helpful. It is important to discipline the urges of food, sex and sleep and not to have fears or to brood on those fears. The sense of self-preservation is very strong in human life. Examine your fears so you realize your mind has created those fears and they are not at all real. If you identify with and brood on fears, you become negative and sad. This is what creates disease.

Everyone eats, but very few people know how to eat for health. Everyone wants to sleep and sleep, but nobody knows how to sleep properly. Everyone wants to do sex, but nobody knows how to control the sexual urge. Training in these basic necessities for human survival and the growth of humanity are not imparted anywhere. This is why there is such chaos in the world. If all human beings were taught how to control sleep, their sleep would be very restful. If all were taught to eat properly—what to eat, how to eat, how much to eat, when to eat and when not to eat—everybody would be healthier. The sexual urge is the most powerful and the most destructive of all sensual desires. If everyone were taught how to control the sexual urge and were made aware of what sex means, there would be fewer marital problems.

Although brahmacharya is often translated as abstinence from sex, or celibacy, in reality it refers to continence in either the celibate or the married state. Sexual excess leads to the dissipation of vital energy that could be used instead to attain deeper states of consciousness. At this point I want to emphasize that brahmacharya should not be interpreted as repression of sensual urges. Repression leads only to frustration and an abnormal state of mind. Brahmacharya means control of and freedom from all sensual cravings. The bliss that accompanies Self-realization is far greater than any transient sensual pleasure, and one whose goal is Self-realization should therefore overcome the obstacles of sensual cravings without the use of suppression. When your mind, actions and emotions are under your control, then you are a brahmachari. One who cultivates brahmacharya is aware of Brahman alone. Such a state is possible only if the mind is free from all sensual desires.

Aparigraha

The practice of the next commitment, *aparigraha,* or nonpossessiveness, is also meant to foster an inward attitude rather than create an outward appearance. Aparigraha does not mean to deny oneself of all material possessions. It involves not being addicted to or dependent on one's possessions rather than the outward denial of them. The danger lies not in having material possessions but in becoming attached to them or in craving more than you need.

Another meaning of aparigraha is not to expect anything from anyone. When you expect too much from others you become dependent on them. Self-reliance is important. Even wife and husband should not become dependant on each other or have too many expectations from each other. Wife says, "I expect you to love me and to listen to me." Husband declares, "I expect you to love me, look after me, serve me and listen to me." You live with each other's expectations, without ever knowing what love is. As long as your expectations are fulfilled, you are both happy. You may live together for thirty years or more and finally realize you have never known each other. This is one of the miseries that society has produced.

What you call love is actually expectation. When two selfish persons expect from each other in the name of love, it is a precarious situation. When you expect too much of your partner, you keep calculating how much you have received from that person. At some point you may decide you have not received enough and so you want a divorce. You should communicate and understand each other by expressing yourself and being honest with each other. If two people who are living together cannot adjust to each other's ego, the relationship falls apart.

It is easy to expect, but very difficult to love. If everyone in the family expects from each other, the family institution will be reduced to a den of selfish people. Expectation is the mother of all problems. To love means to give. Once you learn to give you will receive. That is the law. Today we see the opposite: No one wants to give, but everyone expects to receive. In the world this expectation is considered to be love. Learn to love others unconditionally without any expectation. When you expect too much, you are hurting yourself because you are making yourself dependent on others. You think that to lean on somebody or to expect something from somebody because that person is your friend or spouse is love. This is not true. If you expect happiness from others, you will never have it, because happiness does not come from others. Too much expectation is one of the social miseries humanity is facing today. You expect your partner to be very nice and loving and gentle to you, but what do you expect from yourself? If you get something without expectation, that is okay. But you shouldn't expect it. Pain in the external world comes from too much expectation.

Not everyone can live up to your expectations, and then you feel sad. You depend on others to make you happy, but that type of relationship is superficial. It is better to take time to develop awareness of the center of beauty, wisdom, power and peace that is within you.

Patanjali says there should be one principle in life, one truth. You should focus all your actions, thoughts, desires and emotions toward one aim. You can have many goals, but you should have only one absolute aim. You can marry and have children, a home and enough money to have all the comforts of life, but you should understand that none of these is the ultimate goal in life. It is essential to understand the purpose of life so together you can direct all your resources toward that goal. That is possible if you accept marriage as an opportunity to learn. If you really want to know all the secrets of life, you can learn them at home. You both can become two wheels of the same chariot. Make your husband an instrument for enlightenment, and he can do the same with you. You can have and enjoy all things of the world, but you should apply these as means to reach the ultimate reality. You can live comfortably with a lifespan of one hundred years so you can accomplish the real purpose of life, but it is not helpful to hoard or try to accumulate excessive wealth. When you accumulate wealth, you are exploiting or depriving somebody else. You should not deprive others for your own existence. If you do not have the ultimate reality before you as your goal, other goals will distract you more and more, and instead of giving you pleasure will give you pain. Freedom comes when you learn to love eternal life. Presently you love the objects of your mind and the external world, and you are trying to use God to acquire more and more things. Now you should reverse this process and use the things of the world as a means to achieve your goal and to love the ultimate reality.

These five commitments will give you inner strength and make you a real human being; they will help you to communicate properly with others and to grow in the external world. If you maintain loving relationships with others, you don't lie or steal, you know how to control your energy and you don't accumulate more material wealth than necessary, your relationships in the external world will be more fulfilling. Now there are five more commitments to learn.

The five *niyamas,* or observances, cover more personal aspects of moral discipline. They are *shaucha,* purity or cleanliness of one's body, mind, surroundings and, above all, one's means of livelihood; *santosha* or contentment, which does not mean lack of effort but being content and happy with whatever one acquires after doing one's best, and enjoying it without any complaints or feelings of rivalry or jealousy; *tapas,* or austerity, which incorporates practices that lead to perfection of body, mind and senses; *svadhyaya,* the study of sacred books and the study of one's self, or introspection; and *ishvara pranidhana,* devotion and surrender to God (Brahman), the ultimate reality.

Shaucha

Shaucha means "to cleanse yourself from within, to purify all levels of your being, within and without." Purity of the physical body is very important but shaucha is not limited to the body. Patanjali is referring to purity on all levels — body, breath, senses, mind and spirit. If the body is very sickly, the mind and the spirit will also be affected. When the body is in discomfort and afflicted with disease, the mind and the nervous system remain under stress, and more importantly, it becomes difficult to do spiritual practices.

In the practice of shaucha the first thing to attend to is the body. There is much more to keeping the body clean than taking a bath and brushing the teeth. Four very important organ systems constantly function to purify the body of toxins and wastes: the pores of the skin, the lungs, the kidneys and the bowels. The practice of shaucha on the physical level means to know how to regulate these four systems. The first important step is to allow nature to take its course and not create any obstacle to their natural functioning. If you understand the laws of elimination and purification in your body, you can regulate and assist these natural cleansing systems. They are very important for the overall health of the body and for prevention of disease.

Bad odor and discoloration of the skin are symptoms of ill health, and the use of deodorants and unnatural soaps and lotions or medicines on the skin only hides or suppresses these problems. By suppressing the natural means for ridding the body of toxins with deodorants and other chemical substances, you are only asking for trouble in the future. The extra burden of removing these toxins must then be taken over by the kidneys, causing an excessive strain on them. The pores play a crucial part in cleansing the whole body. The human body was designed to sweat to clean the pores. By interfering with this natural cleansing system you are laying the foundation for ill health. For example, if every night for one week's time you rub a lot of oil on your body and then go to sleep, you will develop a skin disease because the pores will become clogged. Similarly, if you regularly subject your skin to prolonged exposure to sunlight, whether because of your occupation or for the purpose of tanning, you will be at the risk of developing skin cancer.

An ordinary bath cleans the outer layer of the skin but it does not reach deep enough to clean the pores. However, the heat of a steam bath or a sauna bath is very effective in opening and cleaning the pores. In yoga the prana bath is another way to clean the pores. It is better than any external bath. The effects of the prana bath are similar to a steam bath, but in the prana bath the heat is generated internally with the help of pranayama. It is done in the accomplished posture (*siddhasana*) along with uddiyana bandha, mulabandha, *jalandhara bandha* (throat lock) and *antara kumbhaka* (inner retention), in the practice of pranayama. Only advanced students who have learned the method of breath retention from a competent teacher should practise this technique, and it must be executed very carefully and properly so as not to injure the fine tissues of the lungs. This practice was actually developed for those students who live in caves. The student first needs to acquire skill in the preliminary steps of pranayama before attempting the prana bath. It is one of the most effective cleansing techniques known and is highly regarded by the yogis who dwell in the Himalayan Mountains. An unpublished yoga manual, the *Tarangini*, explains the method. The prana bath is briefly described as follows: Contract the diaphragm and exhale completely, without inhaling for some time. This is done repeatedly, according to the capacity of the lungs. This practice should be done only under the guidance of a competent and accomplished teacher.

Besides the prana bath, there are other hatha yoga and pranayama practices such as *mayurasana* (peacock), shirshasana, and *bhastrika* (bellows breathing) that are also very effective in cleansing the pores. In fact, these provide an even more thorough cleansing than can be accomplished by jogging or other forms of vigorous exercise. By controlling the motion of the lungs one can also control the functioning of the pores.

The lungs are obviously important for cleansing the body of toxins. You can live for weeks without food and for days without water, but only minutes without oxygen. Breath is the source of life. It naturally follows that proper breathing is the key to good health.

As you feel very uneasy when your intestines are loaded with roughage, you likewise feel discomfort when you do not properly clean your lungs. If you are in the habit of inhaling oxygen and retaining that oxygen rather than allowing fresh oxygen to come, you are hindering that process. The ultimate aim of breathing exercises is to regulate the motion of the lungs and the input and output of respiratory gases. This is the most effective vital cleansing process. If you regulate the motion of the lungs you can protect yourself from many diseases and maintain a stable emotional balance. The ancients have described varieties of breathing techniques that are useful in producing these effects. These include *nadi shodhanam, kapalabhati, bhastrika* and many others. But the most important practice to help you control the motion of the lungs is diaphragmatic breathing. Breathing diaphragmatically produces a sense of tranquility and reduces stress and tension. This practice is presented in more detail in the section on pranayama, the fourth step of ashtanga yoga.

When you learn to breathe properly you will find that your mind and your thinking become much clearer. By eliminating shallowness, pauses, jerks and noise from your breath, you are assisting the natural process of cleansing the lungs and also helping to cleanse the pores.

The nostrils are very sensitive and important anatomical structures and should be cleansed regularly in order to prevent any obstruction to the flow of breath. One way to do this is *neti kriya*, the nasal wash. This involves cleaning the nostrils by pouring lukewarm saline water first through one nostril and then the other, allowing it to flow out the opposite side. This practice also helps prevent colds, allergies and hay fever.

Prana underlies all the physiological and biochemical reactions of the body. The more you exert yourself physically, the more your muscles consume oxygen and create more carbon dioxide. This exchange takes place in the lungs. Along with the exchange of oxygen and carbon dioxide, there is also an exchange between the prana that is being consumed and that which has already been consumed. Overeating or eating overcooked food or processed food disrupts this exchange, and causes the motion of the lungs as well as the entire respiratory system to become irregular. Even the pores become unable to carry out their cleansing function. If you regulate the motion of the lungs by certain breathing exercises, however, the pores will again function properly and the tissues and cells will return to health.

Prana can also be augmented by the practice of hatha yoga, which prevents any unnecessary loss of energy and helps not only to cleanse the energy body but also to strengthen any weaknesses that may be present in the pranic field.

The kidneys are the toughest filters in the body but they also need natural cleansing every day. The ancients found that the best natural agent to clean the kidneys is whey, the liquid that remains in the simple process of making paneer (fresh cheese): First bring the milk to a boil, squeeze the juice of a lemon into it, and after it curdles, strain it. The clear liquid is the whey. It should not be taken hot. Used regularly, whey is a very good diuretic.

Another way to cleanse the kidneys is to drink enough liquids. This does not include soda pop or alcohol. All carbonated beverages and alcoholic drinks irritate the intestines and leave deposits in the kidneys. Tap water has many chemicals in it, and this too has a similar effect. Natural spring water is good, as well as well water, but the well should be cleaned every year. If water is kept bottled for prolonged periods its properties change, so I don't recommend drinking bottled water.

The best natural liquids you can take are fresh fruit and vegetable juices. A glass of fresh orange juice, cucumber juice or lemon water taken once in the morning, or twice daily if necessary, is very good for cleaning the kidneys. However, when you are thirsty it is better to take pure water than to substitute with juices or bottled water.

The intestines too must be kept clean. If you have to move your bowels, it is obvious that it is not a good thing to delay this process. Sometimes you feel constipated and at other times you may feel the urge for a motion at any time because you have not regulated your bowels. You cannot talk to anyone in a relaxed manner or do your work with a clear mind when the colon is overloaded with roughage. Many intelligent persons, even health professionals, don't know this because nobody has ever taught them.

As far as the bowels are concerned, shaucha means to regulate the movement of the bowels by forming the habit of going to the bathroom on time every day. If you develop the habit of finishing your morning and evening ablutions on time, you will not have to worry about having to go to the bathroom at inconvenient times. It is very important to train yourself to have a bowel movement at the same time every day. This is not difficult to do. Even if the first day you try you do not feel the urge, try again at the same time the next day. After three or four days you will find that your bowels have become regulated. That not only saves time but also helps you to maintain good health. If you have to stay on the toilet for more than five or ten minutes, there is something wrong. Sitting on the toilet for a prolonged period of time unnecessarily can cause hemorrhoids to develop. The causes of constipation are poor food habits, negative thinking and a worried mind.

There is an ancient practice that will help you establish the habit of having a bowel movement the first thing every morning. Squeeze the juice of a normal-sized fresh lemon into a glass of water that has been boiled, and add a pinch of mountain rock salt. When you drink it, the water should be warm, not hot. The salt will help to draw out the waste material from the bloodstream, but only a very small quantity should be used. Adding pure honey to the water will give it a little taste so that it will be easier to drink. An added advantage is that honey is very soothing for the intestines and good for the colon.

After drinking the lemon water you should squat down, feet apart, and place one hand on each knee. Then bring the knees to the floor, one after the other, beside the foot of the opposite leg. As you push one leg to the floor, press the opposite leg against the abdomen, creating a slight pressure on the bowels. After having done this ten to fifteen times you will feel the urge to clear the bowels.

According to yoga science, there are no hard and fast rules as far as food habits are concerned. Yoga does not teach that some foods are allowed and others are not. Any food that is simple and fresh can be part of a healthy diet. Whatever you eat, you should learn to watch your capacity. If there is sufficient roughage in the diet, it will not be difficult to regulate the bowel movement. The best sources of roughage are fresh fruits and vegetables, and whole grains, but not the bran that one buys at the health food store. Such bran is an irritant, though it may be quite effective in maintaining regularity. It is far better to obtain this roughage from whole natural foods, which contain gentler and milder forms of fiber. Drinking milk moderately every day is also very effective in emptying the bowels. Once you have had a bowel movement you should not immediately rush for food.

If you study the etiology of cancer, you will come to know there are certain communities in which you will not find colon cancer because the members do not take soft food and they know how to clean and regulate their bowels. Instead they take food that requires a strong digestive system so the colon does not retain undigested soft things within itself. You have yet to learn this.

Physical purification is not difficult. To build a healthy body you have to cultivate certain habits that will assist the natural cleansing processes of the body. In modern science mucus is considered only as a secretion necessary to line the delicate internal membranes of the internal organs. However, to a yogi, mucus is also an excretion through which the body rids itself of toxins.

The ancients considered excessive quantities of mucus production as a symptom of ill health.

There are certain specific cleansing exercises called kriyas that are described in the ancient yoga manuals for cleaning the internal system. These techniques leave you feeling refreshed and purified of excess mucus and other wastes. To the regular practitioner of yoga they become as important as normal bathing.

The first of these exercises is *kunjal kriya*, the upper wash, which is used to cleanse the stomach and bronchial passages. While squatting, drink about one and a half gallons of lukewarm salted water as rapidly and as steadily as possible, and then throw it up. You should do this on an empty stomach and take only fresh juices afterward.

Dhauti kriya is another exercise that is designed to remove excess mucus from the esophagus and stomach. It involves swallowing a three-inch wide strip of sterilized white cotton cloth that is about twenty feet long. The natural gag reflex helps remove the cloth and mucus rapidly. These techniques may sound difficult at first, but once you have practised them a few times, they become easy. These washes can help you cure many ailments of the lungs and stomach, such as asthma and certain types of indigestion.

In addition there is a system of ductless glands called the endocrine system that plays a very subtle role in the functioning of the body. This system is controlled by the mind. It is called ductless because its secretions go directly into the blood stream. If the endocrine system is not functioning properly, a woman can get irregular menstrual periods. This happens when she becomes emotionally upset. Either it stops completely or it continues indefinitely. When the natural monthly cleansing process of menstruation is interrupted, facial acne and many other problems can occur.

Next comes mental purity. Mental purification is possible and is very essential. Internal strength comes from purification of the mind. Purity of mind means nothing disturbs you. A pure mind is free of all conflicts, whether they come from family life, business, personal habits or from mere ignorance. To achieve a state of mental purity you have to cultivate *smriti* (mindfulness) and discrimination. The first step is to become aware of your thoughts. Through constant awareness you can learn to discriminate between pure and impure thoughts on the basis of whether they lead to greater freedom or greater bondage and ignorance. You are what you are because of the way you think, feel and understand. It is not helpful to have animosity toward others or to imagine negative things. Negative thinking cannot be washed away by soap and water. If you are constantly blasted by your thoughts, it means you are identifying with them. If you can be an objective witness to your thinking process, adverse, negative or passive thoughts will not affect you. Listen to your conscience. It will tell you if your thoughts, speech and actions are right. When there is coordination between your actions and speech and between your speech and mind, you are thinking right. If you think in your mind that something is not right and yet you do it anyway, that creates conflict. The mind keeps brooding on those experiences that create conflict in the mind. It is better for you to be free from conflicts by not allowing your mind to brood over or contemplate conflicting negative ideas. To purify your mind of conflicts first of all you should sit down and examine the conflicts you have. You have not resolved them because you have been afraid to face yourself. Sooner or later you will have to put an end to those fears so there will be no conflict. Confusion comes from within, from the mind or the intellect. It does not come from any external source. When you are confused it is either because you have not purified the mind or you have not sharpened the buddhi.

Similarly, environmental pollution comes from thought pollution. You will have to take the responsibility to change yourself in order to stop the environmental crises you have created for yourself and others. In this busy society it is essential to learn certain breathing techniques and meditation. These practices will help to calm down the mind and are part of the purification process.

The Book of Revelation in the Bible is not a book that just anyone could have written. Even though John was not one of the disciples of the great master, Jesus Christ, the revelations came through him because he was pure in heart, mind and soul. Pure in heart means he had no emotional problems; pure in mind means his mind was free of conflicts; and his individual soul was searching for its summum bonum, as the river searches for the ocean.

In the path of sadhana, preparation is very important. You have to prepare yourself and discipline yourself. Don't allow anyone to impose disciplines on you. Prepare your mind to be one-pointed and then surrender that one-pointed mind. You cannot surrender a scattered mind that you have not yet mastered. The ancient sages became great because they prepared themselves to receive knowledge. They became great instruments because their minds and hearts were pure. You also can purify your mind and heart exactly as they did. Once your mind is made one-pointed and inward, such a purified mind has the power to lead you closer to Atman. Sincerity and perseverance are essential to cultivate shaucha. When shaucha is perfected, the yogi shrinks from his body and avoids the touch of others.

Santosha

The next commitment is *santosha*, or contentment. There is a difference between satisfaction and contentment. You should never be satisfied, yet you should always be content. If you remain satisfied, you will not be motivated to do anything. But if you don't do anything and don't want to do anything yet you say you are content, then you will have to be prepared to accept the consequences. If you do your work according to your full capacity and skills, you should be content to accept whatever you receive from your actions. Your effort should stem from a sense of duty and service instead of from discontent or anticipation of the fruits of your efforts.

A person's desires are insatiable. No sooner is one fulfilled than another arises, causing the mind to remain in a constant state of agitation. Tranquility is possible only through the cultivation of santosha. But contentment should not lead to slackening of effort.

If you do not know contentment you can never be peaceful or happy. You may try to create happiness by establishing ownership of people and things, but as long as you look for happiness in the external world, you will remain unhappy. The external world can keep you busy but it cannot give you happiness. You are so attached to the world that you identify with the objects of the world in such a way that you allow them to control your life.

In this way you have become a victim. Once you get attached to the things of the world you remain caught in a whirlpool and you are miserable. Actually the objects of the world are only means to help you achieve the goal of Self-realization. When those means are helpful to you, you love them, because it is easy to love objects of joy. But if the same means become painful or create obstacles for you, you no longer love them and they are no longer helpful.

You can have the best of all the means but unless you have the right attitude towards life and you understand what the purpose of life is, you will never be happy. You keep yourself busy by eating, drinking and enjoying the things of the world without understanding why you are doing these things. If you want to follow the worldly path of action to attain Self-realization you have to perform your duties lovingly and skillfully, and reject all claims of ownership and attachment to the objects of the world.

Those who are truly content remain happy, no matter where they are. It is said that a crown and its accompanying kingdom and riches would be a useless burden for a fakir, because he is already content and has no need for these things. For those who think they need name and fame and worldly wisdom, Patanjali advises instead selfless and skillful action while remaining content. No matter what happens you should be joyous all the time. Those who are wise say you can be eternally happy, even in the worst conditions. It is possible to enjoy life in all situations. When you forget this, you sink into the grooves of your past habits and become sad. Even though your true nature is happiness, you are not happy because you are emotionally imbalanced. If you get what you want, you become emotional and cannot enjoy the situation. When you do not get what you want, you sink into depression. You can learn to enjoy all situations when you know how to create and maintain a state of inner tranquility. The way of adjustment leads to contentment. Live in the external world but compose yourself and remain with the center all the time. In this way you can be at peace within and without. Don't create unhappiness for yourself by leaning on external resources for happiness. Life is a learning process. You will always be happy if you remain constantly with the friend within. This is the karma yoga way of doing actions in the world, the way of karma.

The path of action in the world is as perfect as the path of renunciation. If you learn the technique of living in the world and yet remaining above, you will have no reason to think that you are incapable or incompetent. You have all the resources within, yet you remain unsatisfied and unfulfilled because you are utilizing very few of these resources. You can use the means in the external world and all the resources within to attain Self-realization. No swami, yogi, temple or any person can ever give you happiness. Only you can give happiness to yourself, and that happiness comes when you have understood how to live in the external world. The best formula for the external world is: *All the things of the world that have been given to me are means. I should not allow them to create barriers for me to attain enlightenment.* Do your duties without being attached to the results and with full love.

The most important aspect of human health is to be free mentally. Cheerfulness is the greatest of all physicians. Don't forget that you have come for only a short while to this platform. Be free and build your own philosophy and don't allow anything to disturb you. If you know how to apply all the means of the world to attain the purpose of life, you will know happiness both in the external world and within. It is rare to find someone who is happy from within. Most people's happiness is ephemeral because it is dependent on the external world. Real happiness is a state of mind where you are free from all pains and miseries.

Tapas

After santosha comes *tapas*, or austerity. The practice of tapas helps to destroy impurities and awaken physical and mental powers. The word *tapas* has often been wrongly interpreted as excessive austerity and mortification of the flesh, as exemplified by the hair shirt and bed of nails. But in the Bhagavad Gita, Lord Krishna clearly states that yoga is not for one who either indulges the flesh or tortures it. In the practice of yoga tapas has nothing to do with the denial of the necessities of life. Necessities are different from the seemingly endless wants and needs that merely serve to dissipate your mental and physical powers. The necessities of life are few and simple. To practise tapas means to live with the simple necessities of life.

Tapas can also be interpreted as control of the senses. Mind does not run to the external world by itself. It depends on the five gross senses and the five subtle senses. The five gross senses are the capacities to speak, to work with the hands, to move with the feet, to procreate and to eliminate. The subtle senses are five distinct channels of the mind that flow toward the objects of the external world: seeing, hearing, touching, smelling and tasting. The senses are the channels through which the mind identifies itself with the objects of the world. The charms, temptations and attractions of the world are so powerful that they continually dissipate the mind and draw it to the external world. Mind wants to relish and enjoy all the sense experiences of the external world, even though some are joyous and others are painful. The moment you wake up you are bombarded by sense perceptions: either you see, hear, sense or remember. You speak in the language of thought forms and identify with the objects of the world. This is why it is very difficult to prepare the mind to do research in the interior world. It does not want to go to the world of abstract knowledge because it is not very sure what it is going to experience. When you try to convince the mind to do meditation, it will play tricks on you and find many excuses not to go within. People who do not know how to go beyond the mire of the senses inevitably suffer.

You do not see things as they are nor as you want to see them, but as your senses allow you to see them. You are what you think, so it is important to be able to perceive the way you want to perceive. In addition, even if you have clarity of mind, the data that is being supplied to your senses is not proper because everything in the world is subject to change, death and decay. It is difficult to study something whose nature keeps changing.

The practice of tapas helps you to become an insider by controlling your mind and senses. This will help you to understand the purpose of life and to become creative and dynamic so you can serve humanity. There are many different practices to help you develop control over the senses. The first step is to become aware of your conscience, the teacher within that is ever present and ever willing to offer guidance. This does not mean you should no longer listen to your external teacher, but it is the responsibility of that teacher to make you aware of the teacher and great friend within. Slowly your teacher will make you independent, because it is the tendency of human beings to become dependent on the teacher. And if a teacher allows that dependency, then he is nowhere and the student is nowhere, and they live like slave and master. Your first teacher is actually your conscience. Because you tend to ignore your conscience, it has become silent and merely witnesses your actions. If you start to listen to your conscience, you will become very close to the reality.

The practice of tapas is also evident in the great religions. Whether you are doing puja in a temple or attending a mass in a Catholic church, the rituals have many similarities and the same objects are used to focus the attention of the senses: the sound of the bells and chanting, the burning of incense and the visual images of the gods. The reason these objects are used is to keep the senses occupied so they do not distract the mind. Once you satisfy and pacify all the senses, it is easier to go into a state of meditation.

When you are successful in the practice of tapas and the system of ashtanga yoga, your mind becomes very clear and you see things as they are, without conflict or deception. Clarity of mind is very important not only to be successful in the world, but also to attain divinity. The practice of tapas can help you to have access to the tremendous power of your mind. One of India's former prime ministers, Morarji Desai, was a perfect example of what can be achieved through tapas. He became prime minister at the age of seventy-nine, by which age many people are suffering from senility. But he remained very active and intelligent and he was very strong. I knew him personally so I can relate these things to you. He was arrested during the emergency that had been declared by Indira Gandhi. When the police came to arrest him, he said, "I have not yet completed my meditation. Please wait until I have done so, then you can take me."

One of the policemen grabbed his arm roughly and told him he had to come just then. Morarji Desai then caught hold of the arms of both policemen simultaneously and twisted them until both men fell down to the ground. He then said to them, "Listen, the two of you are not strong enough to take me by force. You will have to call for more help if you want to take me."

It was his habit to get up at 3 o'clock in the morning to practise yoga and meditation up to 7 o'clock, the time during which everyone usually remains sleeping. Those four hours he wouldn't give to any one. When he walked, he walked like a king. It is possible for the body to remain strong and healthy as you grow older if you regularly devote some time to taking care of it. When you start to work with your body you will come to know you are dealing with far more than just the body.

Tapas literally means "that which generates heat," for heat arises in a person who has a burning zeal for enlightenment. I have always experimented a lot and many times my experiments took me even to the verge of death and loss of consciousness. I knew I could not attain enlightenment merely by reading the teachings of others and that I had to enlighten myself, as Buddha had taught.

A simple life, free from sensual indulgence, focused on chanting the name of the Lord and serving one's fellow human beings, constitutes tapas. Through tapas one develops not only strength of body and mind but also enhanced spiritual zeal. Tapas is closely connected to the next commitment, svadhyaya. The practice of tapas helps you to discipline yourself and frees your mind from the distractions of the external world so you can study yourself within.

Svadhyaya

Svadhyaya is study that leads to knowledge of the Self. It encompasses the study of the scriptures and other books of spiritual value, and includes not only the study of the lives and teachings of the great sages who have guided humanity in the past but more importantly, self-study.

It is not sufficient to study good books because they are based on the opinion of others. The study of books may help you to develop cognition, but it will not help you to become aware of the different levels of consciousness. Your education focuses on only one aspect of life, the external world. You study the minutest details of things in the external world but you do not know how to study your own nature. At one time I also was caught up in education in the external world:

Because I had a great desire to learn languages, I kept trying to learn more and more. Finally, one day my master asked, "Why are you doing this?"

I replied, "I want to know at least thirty-four languages and read thousands of books."

In order to accomplish this I had taught myself how to do speed-reading. It's a very simple thing. If you have a one-pointed mind and you understand something about memory, you can easily do it.

He said, "Look, I am going to tell you a true story. There was a great man who was very wealthy and had only one son. The people honored that man very much and expected his son to be exactly like him, or better than him. When the time came for his son to attend university, he sent him abroad for higher education. Eventually he passed his master's degree in fourteen subjects. That man is still alive in India. It was common to see his name in the newspaper, announcing that he was doing yet another master's degree. When he returned home after this achievement he no longer spoke to his father gently or affectionately as he had previously.

"How are you, Father?" he asked mechanically.

His father was disturbed to see the changes that had taken place in him and asked him, "What has happened to you? Which MA have you done this time?"

"I have done it in history."

His father advised, "Ask your teachers, those who have taught you, if they have known themselves. What is the use of knowing many subjects if you have not known yourself? Go back and put this question to your teachers."

When he returned to the university he did as requested by his father. They all responded similarly: "I do not know!"

He was disappointed and went back to report to his father. He told him he was sorry but none of his teachers knew anything about knowing oneself. His father asked, "Then what is the use of knowing all these subjects and languages?"

I understood what my master was trying to teach me. Immediately I stopped the pursuit of book knowledge and language acquisition. Now I speak the universal language called broken English.

Svadhyaya is not limited to the study of a particular subject or huge books. The knowledge of worldly things will never help you, no matter how much you know. But for attaining spiritual heights it is helpful to study all the great religions of the world and all the noble spiritual traditions so you can form your own opinion and decide which is best for you. They are all based on one and the same truth and have come from the same great light to comfort and lead mankind. The practical methods of whichever tradition you have chosen will help you attain your goal. While treading the path, individuals from different traditions may have different experiences, but on reaching the summit, everyone will have the same vision.

At some point you will reach the stage where you will become tired of studying things in the external world, and you will realize that now you have to study yourself. Unfortunately, this realization often comes very late. In old age the mind remains preoccupied and is not prepared to understand, store to memory and to recall new information.

The first step is not to know God, but to know yourself. When you say you want to know God, it means you are searching for something without truly understanding it. It is sure you will not meet God anywhere because you don't yet understand what you are trying to do. You should first know yourself on all levels. The study of the self is the highest of all studies. The self is not limited to body, senses and mind. No matter which path you tread, you have to understand yourself on all levels within and without before you can know God. Study your thoughts, speech, actions and your emotions and desires; study your internal states, motivations and the outward flow of your senses.

Whatever you know about yourself, others have told you. You have not yet known anything original about yourself. You are a stranger to yourself and that is the cause of your suffering. When you study yourself from within you will find you are entirely different than what you thought you were. Then you will no longer identify with the body or the environment in which you live.

When you decide to know yourself you can start by studying your actions and developing awareness of your body language. Whatever you are doing you have habitual ways of carrying your body, positioning your body and making gestures. This is called body language. Observe how your body changes and how free it feels when you are joyful and how it tenses and contracts when you are angry. Learn to question your actions and see if your conscience approves of your actions.

You can begin the study of your mind by examining the conscious mind. Observe what is going on in your mind and find out what it is that makes you emotional. Examine the habit patterns that make up your personality and try to find how you formed those habits. If you make effort you can undo habit patterns by training your mind to create new grooves so it no longer flows to the old grooves. This is the way to completely transform your personality. It takes a lot of effort and discipline. Discipline means to do something with full attention and understanding of what you are doing and why you are doing it. Self-study is not possible without attention. The very root of the ashtanga system is attention — how to pay attention towards one thing one-pointedly.

The greatest obstacle to progress on the path is self-condemnation. In the process of self-study, it is important to remember not to condemn yourself or to become egotistical. Don't condemn yourself no matter how bad or how small you are, because there is always a chance to grow. Whenever you encounter negative thought patterns, you tend to immediately start to condemn yourself because you identify with your thought patterns. Nothing in you is bad, but you condemn yourself because you are not aware that there is something higher and glorious within yourself. If you continue to identify with negative thought patterns, you will never be able to come in touch with the reality within. Don't accept it if your mind tells you that you are good for nothing. Don't become defensive and egotistical over little things or build boundaries around yourself. If you observe your thoughts, you will notice that you often blame others for your difficulties. When this happens, question why your mind tends to focus on others' negative actions and speech, and why you keep brooding over negative events.

Question why you think you are miserable and that everybody else is also miserable. Try to understand why you think negatively even though you don't want to, and why you condemn yourself. When you are negative you become weak and frightened, and your mind can imagine many things. You can even feel that somebody is twisting your neck, or create a ghost that is not there. It means you are weak if you identify with the objects of your thinking process.

One of the main causes of self-condemnation is that instead of forming your own opinion, you live and act on the opinions of others. In your relationships in the world, you are so controlled by the opinions of others that you assume their opinions as your personality. This is a sickness. If you allow the world to be your mirror, your whole life and personality will be determined by the opinions of others. Accept yourself as you are but keep working with yourself. Don't suddenly become upset if somebody says you look ugly. Don't become confused if one person says you are good and another says you are bad. Likewise don't expect others to praise you all the time and tell you that you are beautiful and wonderful. Learn not to be affected by or swayed by others' opinions. It is a weakness to depend on external sources. Learn to admire yourself rather than depending on appreciation and admiration from others. You are depending on external sources that are giving you fake suggestions and allowing your life to be controlled by those fake suggestions. You always look to others to know about yourself and to understand who you are. Now form your own opinion and see yourself as you are. If you don't begin to turn over the pages of the book of inner life, the study of the external world will only confuse you more. If you learn to admire and appreciate life, you will not be affected by external influences or opinions of others. Just be what you are and don't try to pretend to be what you are not.

Self-study means to know yourself as you are on all levels. It will help you to encounter both the superficial complexes and the deeper potentials within you. If you allow those potentials to come forward in a creative way you can become dynamic in the external world and help others. But if you continue to identify with your thought patterns, you will only be aware of your superficial self. To know yourself means to know all the levels of your mind, including the unconscious and higher levels. If you know yourself it will become easier for you to understand and communicate with others, and to understand life and its relationships. Without understanding life you cannot understand relationship. Since you do not know yourself, it is hard for you to communicate with others or to understand the feelings and emotions and desires of others. If at all you know yourself, you know yourself through others. You have never taken the time or opportunity to understand yourself independently. Relationship does not just mean how you are related in the external world. More importantly it means how body, breath, conscious mind and unconscious mind are all related and how they function together.

In the prayer, *Lead me from the unreal to the real,* the word *unreal* does not mean the world does not exist. The world exists. It is unreal because all the things of the world are subject to change, death and decay. What you see today, you will find in a different shape and form tomorrow. As long as you identify yourself with the changing objects of the world, you will not understand who you really are. You identify with your thoughts and this is the root of all miseries. You have to understand your mind by understanding your thinking. I will tell you a definite way to understand yourself. I am talking of the relationship between your body and soul. Now, pay attention to this dialogue:

"Well Sir, where is that soul? I don't find any reason to try to understand or to believe in the soul."

"But have you tried to understand that power that you are using for thinking, listening, understanding and discriminating? What is that power? From where does it come?"

"It probably comes from the mind. Why should I believe in the soul?"

"Do you mean to say the mind is all powerful? Have you not observed how your mind is always changing? How can something that is subject to change be called truth? Truth is that which never changes. Truth was there previously; it is here now, and it will remain in the future. If mind is to be considered the source, the fountainhead of power and light, then mind should not change. But if you analyze the mind you will see that mind is constantly changing: you change your opinions, your judgments and even the way you think. Mind is only an instrument that has the capacity to fathom a very small part of the light and life that is present in the power of the soul. If part of a steel bar is being heated, the rest of it also becomes hot. So is the case with the mind. The power that radiates through mind, the power to judge and think, does not belong to mind. Mind is only an instrument. There is something beyond mind that is giving power to mind."

"Well Sir, then is mind matter?"

"No. You don't understand the difference between the mind and the brain. The brain is the seat of the mind. Mind is energy. The nervous system is the channel through which the mind works."

A scientific study of the physical brain cannot tell us much about the nonphysical energy that is activating it. Just as mind is different from the brain, mind is also not identical to the soul. From the soul the mind receives the power to move, and likewise the body gets the power to function from the mind. The mind is constantly changing, but the soul is not subject to change, death and decay because the soul is immortal. The greatest wonder of the world is that this finite, mortal vessel carries infinity within it. Wherever you go, wherever you move, the Lord of life is always with you. If this is true, you may wonder why you are suffering so much. From childhood onward you have been taught to see and examine things in the external world, but nobody has taught you how to search within. Up to now what you have learned is not real knowledge. You should develop confidence based on the fact that the absolute truth is omnipresent and omniscient and therefore within you also. For strengthening that confidence there are three schools: prayer, contemplation and meditation. All three are valid and can help you to cultivate the inner strength to help you dispel the darkness of ignorance.

If you are eager to come in touch with the higher knowledge, you will have to take time to understand yourself. Stop depending on others and on external objects for happiness. If you want happiness, peace and wisdom, it is necessary to understand mind in its totality. Mind is not as small as you think. Mind is the wall between you and the reality. If you understand this wall, you will be free forever.

On the path to enlightenment you have to follow a system to know yourself. The more you know yourself the more you will realize how close you are to the Lord of life. As long as you continue to run away from yourself and try to escape from the realities of life, you will be denying yourself the benefits that come with higher knowledge. Even after extensive self-study you may realize that what you know about yourself is still not enough, and so you may again feel the need to search for something or someone to guide you. When you reach the point of exhaustion, suddenly a sage may come and ask:

"Why are you so sad?"

"I have been searching for something for many years but have not yet found it, even though I have searched everywhere."

"Fool, close your eyes. What you are searching for is within you. "

Ishvara pranidhana

The fifth niyama is *ishvara pranidhana*. The Lord that dwells within everyone is *Ishvara,* that purusha or center of consciousness who is sleeping within the city of life. You are aware of the known part of life: body, senses and mind with its various functions. But you are not aware of the center of consciousness within because ego limits your awareness to the small self. *Ishvara* is "that which directly controls your life," and *pranidhana* means "to let ego become aware of the reality and surrender to it." Patanjali is reminding us there is something beyond ego. He is not telling you to surrender your ego before the world, because if you do this, you will not be able to survive. You should surrender your mere self or ego only before the real Self, the Lord within you. Body, senses, mind and the various functions of mind, ego and intellect comprise the known part of life. But you do not know Ishvara, who is sleeping in the city of life. You should surrender your ego, which separates you from the reality and does not allow you to expand your consciousness. Make your ego inward so that it becomes aware of Ishvara, the controller of the life force. Then consciousness can flow freely from its source.

Learn to trust in the higher power, but not totally. It is okay to utilize and trust in human resources up to a point, but it is dangerous to totally rely on human resources. Likewise, if you do not trust in human resources at all and make no effort, you are committing a great crime against the Lord of life because you are not utilizing the power and resources He has given to you.

The ego has forgotten it is actually a representative of Ishvara. That is why you become egotistical and build boundaries around yourself. In this state you don't communicate with others and you become confused. The ego creates so many obstacles for you that nobody can help you. When you lock yourself within the bounds of ego you become egotistical and you are not open to advice or teaching from anyone, nor can you study anything. In my youth my ego often presented a great challenge to my master:

I used to jump in the Ganges at Rishikesh and swim and float all the way to Haridwar, which was fourteen miles away. My master had warned me several times not to do this.

I replied arrogantly, "I don't have a mother. The Ganges is my only mother and she would never harm me."

"Don't boast in front of me. Listen to what I am telling you."

"Why should I listen to you when I am an excellent swimmer?"

Then he acquiesced and said, "Okay."

Shortly after that I decided to swim to Hari ki Pauri at Haridwar, the place where *aarti* is done every evening at sunset. It was rainy season so the river was flowing forcefully and before I could reach my destination I found myself caught in a whirlpool. Many people were watching me from the banks of the river, but nobody could help me. After being tossed around the whirlpool three times I realized there was no chance for me to survive. As a last resort I remembered my master and promised I would always listen to him if he would help me. Of course he rescued me again and when I met him he said, "I hope you are not going to break your promise ever again. Please don't keep troubling me like this."

Many times my master asked me, "Why are you not trying to understand me?"

Sometimes I was just behaving childishly, and sometimes my lack of comprehension was genuine. He said, "I keep trying to give you wisdom, but you cannot retain it because there is a hole in your head."

I said, "I cannot see the hole. If you can see the hole, why do you not patch it?"

"You are a modern boy and you don't know how to stoop, so you cannot fetch water."

For stooping you have to bow. You don't know how to bow because you are suffering from a serious ego problem. You feed your ego and your ego makes you lonely and separates you from the whole. You think there is nothing within beyond ego. You talk to your ego all the time and think you are gaining knowledge. You say you are praying but instead you are feeding your ego. You become egocentric and think it is growth. You're not fit for yourself because you don't know the totality of yourself; you're not fit for others because you are selfish and egotistical. But I am not totally condemning ego. Individual ego is needed to take care of the body, but it is incorrect to claim, "This is *my* body." Ishvara is the real proprietor of your life and body. Your body, senses and mind all belong to God. The part of ego that maintains your body is very helpful, but when it does not allow you to go beyond body consciousness it inhibits your growth and consequently you suffer.

Ego is aware of only two things — *I* and *mine*. Ego can be a means but it is not the end. If you refine your ego it will become a means to know the reality. You should use your ego as you use your shoes. Your shoes are useful for you if you use them until they are worn out. They are of no use if you polish them and put them in the cupboard. Similarly many people buy a new car and polish it so much they are afraid to use it and keep it locked in the garage. Either you should learn to wear out your ego as you wear your shoes in the external world, or you should polish it and sharpen it so that ego becomes a means for Self-realization. Both things are possible when you start to become aware of the reality behind ego. Then you will be able to make the best use of ego.

If you think ego is the end, your mind will remain within the boundary of ego, where you are not open to advice or teaching. If somebody praises you, all the praises should go to the Lord, because all that is good and great belongs to the Lord. Don't be tossed by your ego or feed your ego when praises come to you. Remember you are being praised because of the life force within you. Don't accept it personally. Surrender your ego to the Lord. Self-surrender is one of the highest ways of living. The real you is a light. Surrender your ego before that light.

You cannot live in the world without relationships, no matter how much you isolate yourself. You are not meant to live for yourself alone. If you say you are studying yoga for yourself and not for anybody else, this attitude will only lead you to a very egotistical way of life. It is true that the whole world is meant for you to use, but you should understand that you are also meant for the world. You can use the things of the world, and at the same time do your actions for others, maintaining an attitude of peace within and without.

The shortest cut to enlightenment is to cut the ego. Even though you may sincerely want to expand the horizon of your mind, it is not so easy to cut the ego. Ego is afraid your individuality will be threatened and feels insecure because it doesn't know what is going to happen in the future. There is no reason to be afraid. When a drop of water meets the ocean, it doesn't lose its identity; it becomes the ocean. Learn to surrender your ego, not before the world or the objects of the world, but before Ishvara who is sleeping within the city of life. That seed contains everything. If you allow it to awaken and grow, it will destroy the knot of ignorance that creates bondage for you and gives you many fears, pain and miseries. The ego has great tenacity and resists such complete surrender, but by transcending the ego you can attain knowledge of your true nature. Then you will be able to do wonders in the world. To surrender the ego means to accept the higher reality. It does not mean to renounce the ego. You can do it in this lifetime. Your essential nature is the same as purusha. Once you have accepted this truth and have surrendered your ego, consciousness can flow freely from its source.

In the context of spiritual pracice, *pranidhana* means "to be aware of and depend on Ishvara, the source of light, love and life within you." There is no need to go to the temple and do rituals. Rituals and external worships are in vain if you have not done something to understand Ishvara, the Lord of life within. Ishvara pranidhana, total surrender to the ultimate reality, is possible only if you have infinite faith and dedication and practise over a long period of time with sincerity and perseverance.

In the Gita, Krishna beautifully explains to Arjuna: *ishvarah sarvabhutanam hriddesho'rjuna tishthai:* O Arjuna, Ishvara is present in that place which is the heart of all beings. (Bhagavad Gita, 18.61)

God is omnipresent, omniscient and omnipotent. Therefore look within, to the deeper states of your being, for God is also there. If God is everywhere, He must be in you and me. And if He is within, He is there in full majesty.

This is the foundation of meditation.

If you learn to depend on the Lord of life within, you can live in the world yet remain above it. *Devatma-shakti* is the direct light coming from the kingdom of the Lord within. A yogi devoid of all impurities can see the light within. By coming in touch with this light, a yogi purifies himself of all samskaras, and is free. The highest yoga is liberation through self-surrender.

There is no need to feel overwhelmed by the seemingly immense task of applying the yamas and niyamas to your daily life. You are not expected to attain instant perfection in the practice of these restraints and observances. It is better to regard the yamas and niyamas as ideals towards which you work with sincerity, while attempting to follow them to the fullest extent possible. Don't give up when you feel discouraged. Rather, use each failure as motivation for future success. Gradually you will become aware that even a small degree of success will help to reduce the intensity of emotional upheavals and mental distractions.

After incorporating the ten commitments of the first two rungs of ashtanga yoga into your daily life, next is to learn how to use the physical body to assist you in the inward journey. If the physical body creates disturbance, you will not be able to meditate.

First Learn to Sit STILL

Asana is the Sanskrit word for "posture." In the Yoga Sutras Patanjali has not described asana or pranayama in detail. It was later that the exponents of hatha yoga integrated it into ashtanga yoga because they realized that a sickly body and dissipated mind are obstacles to progress in ashtanga yoga. Since hatha yoga helps to ensure physical health and mental balance, which are prerequisites for concentration and meditation, it has become both an auxiliary to ashtanga yoga and an essential part of it.

There are two categories of asanas: the first includes those for physical well-being, and the second consists of those for meditation. For a detailed discussion of the former, consult a manual on hatha yoga. Here Patanjali is referring to the latter, the meditative postures. However, for modern humanity, a basic knowledge of hatha yoga is essential to prepare the body to be able to sit. Otherwise it will be difficult to remain in any of the meditation postures for an extended time.

Those who want to tread the path of yoga seriously and successfully should follow the order and the scientific process expounded by experienced yogis who have done research internally. They found that first it is necessary to learn to sit still. After examining many postures they concluded that a meditative posture should meet the following criteria: The head, neck and trunk should be aligned, allowing the natural curves of the spine, and it should be steady and comfortable.

By keeping your head, neck and trunk aligned you are allowing the three major nadis or energy channels, *ida, pingala* and *sushumna*, located along the spinal cord, to function efficiently. If you do not keep the body perfectly aligned, the energy flow will become obstructed, and the body will begin to tremble after a few minutes, causing disturbance to the mind. Besides the interruption to the flow of energy, there will be additional adverse effects on the physical level: The gland centers that are situated along the spinal column will be deprived of adequate blood supply. This restriction of the blood circulation will interfere with the functioning of the respiratory system and you will find it difficult to breathe in a natural way. In order to prevent these problems the ancient adepts formulated some guidelines and four main sitting postures for practising breathing exercises, pranayama, concentration and meditation.

To begin with, your meditation seat should be wooden, not steel, and fully cushioned. It is helpful to use a wooden plank because wood is not a good conductor of electricity and it isolates you from the environment. Never use the bed because it will create problems for your spinal column. Similarly a spongy cushion is too imbalanced and this can be injurious to you. It is better to fold a blanket to a height that is suitable to your level of flexibility. Place the blanket on a wooden floor or plank in a quiet room where you will not be disturbed.

Next choose a posture that is comfortable and at the same time steady. Be honest with yourself and be aware of your capacity. When choosing a meditation posture, do not make yourself sit in a position in which you are not comfortable or for which you have not adequately prepared yourself. If you force your body into an uncomfortable position you may injure a muscle, tendon or ligament.

The classical asanas, or sitting postures, suitable for pranayama, concentration and meditation are: *padmasana* (lotus pose), *siddhasana* (accomplished posture), *svastik-asana* (auspicious posture) and *sukhasana* (easy posture). Many of you think you are great if you can sit in the lotus posture, and the next day you have to go to the doctor for a muscle pull. Posture does not mean you have to twist your limbs or hurt yourself. The upper and lower limbs have very little to do with a meditation posture except to act as supports to the body. But they should be under your control and placed in a position where they don't disturb you or result in the outflow of energy. The overall effect of the seated posture is to slow down the activity of the heart and lungs and lessen the disturbance of the physical body on the mind. This in turn greatly aids concentration. If you are not accustomed to sitting this way, you may find that after a short time your body will slowly revert to your habitual posture. With determination and regular practice, you will be able to master the sitting posture that is suitable for you.

Although padmasana is included as one of the classical asanas for meditation, for practical purposes it is not ordinarily used as a meditative posture. Instead it is practised to help develop flexibility in the lower extremities. Someone who is an adept in the practice of hatha yoga could probably master padmasana as a meditative posture, but because the anal sphincter is relaxed in this pose, it is difficult to create and maintain mulabandha, the root lock. Also it is not easy to sit correctly and comfortably in this posture for an extended length of time. This is why advanced students prefer siddhasana.

The best posture for meditation is siddhasana. Highly accomplished yogis usually master siddhasana, and do not recommend any other sitting posture. In siddhasana it is easy to apply mulabandha and lock it with your heel. Slowly and gently, if you have good guidance and if you sincerely practice, you will be able to make siddhasana comfortable and steady.

Traditionally siddhasana is taught to advanced students, and is not generally recommended as a posture for general use. It requires the ability to put the body into a particular position that is only helpful if it is done precisely and correctly. If one does not have the flexibility to completely attain the posture and maintain it comfortably, it will not bring about the intended benefits and can even create some difficulties or disturbances for the student. It is not recommended for beginners or for those who live in the world. Those who have decided to lead a deep, meditative life should practise this posture. When an advanced student can sit in this pose for more than three hours at a time, without any aches or pains, it is said that *asana siddhi* (proficiency in asana) has been acquired.

To sit in siddhasana place the left heel at the perineum (the region between the anus and the genitals) after applying mulabandha. This is done by contracting the anal sphincter muscles and pulling them inward. Then place the other heel at the pubic bone above the organ of generation. Arrange the feet and legs so that the ankles are positioned one on top of the other. Insert the toes of the right foot between the left thigh and calf so that only the big toe is visible; then pull up the toes of the left foot between the right thigh and calf so that the big toe is visible. Now place your hands on your knees with the thumbs and respective index fingers touching. You should practise this posture only if you have learned it under direct personal guidance, because it can create difficulties if it is not done correctly.

Yogis use siddhasana to sit for meditation and to awaken the *kundalini* (the dormant energy of Shakti). It is also helpful to gain control of the sexual urge. One who can sit in this pose for a long time will be less distracted by this urge, because siddhasana directly affects muladhara, the sacral plexus, and the secretion of hormones of the testes and ovaries. That is why this meditative posture is helpful for renunciates. One who lives in the world should not sit in siddhasana for more than half an hour at a time, whereas a renunciate should maintain the pose for more than two hours and five minutes. If you can sit for two and a half hours in this posture you will no longer feel any pain, and when you come out of the posture you will feel normal. Yoga has many ways to control and to be free from physical pain.

If your legs are flexible enough, you may find it more comfortable to sit in svastikasana for longer periods of meditation. Because this posture has a wider foundation, it distributes the body weight more directly on the floor and is somewhat steadier and less likely to lead to swaying or other bodily movements. In this posture the knees rest directly on the floor rather than on the feet, so there is less weight or pressure on the ankles. To come into svastikasana sit comfortably on your meditation seat, then bend the left leg at the knee and place the left foot alongside the right thigh. Place the sole of the left foot flat against the inside of the right thigh. Next, bend the right knee and place the sole of the right foot against the left thigh, so the right foot is between the thigh and the back of the left calf and the toes are tucked in. Then take the toes of your left foot up between the right thigh and calf until the big toe is visible. This creates a very symmetrical, comfortable and stable posture, which is very effective for meditation. Svastikasana is especially recommended for women.

If you a beginner and are not used to sitting on the floor and thus find the above three postures to be too painful or uncomfortable, you can start with either sukhasana or *maitreyasana* (friendship pose). Sukhasana is a simple, cross-legged position that is done as follows: Place each foot on the floor under the opposite knee and rest each knee on the corresponding opposite foot. If your hips are not flexible enough to maintain the natural curves and alignment of the spine in this posture, you should fold a blanket to the required height and put it underneath the buttocks. This will allow the pelvis to tip forward slightly, which alleviates the pressure on the knees and ankles.

It is also quite permissible for beginners, or those who experience difficulty sitting in the time-honored postures, to sit erect in a straight-backed chair, placing the hands on the knees or thighs, keeping the head, neck and trunk aligned and the feet flat on the floor. This is maitreyasana. Beginners who have not yet acquired flexibility in the hips and knees, older individuals and persons with physical disabilities that prevent them from sitting on the floor, can use maitreyasana.

The following are some general suggestions regarding the sitting postures: You will probably find initially that once you have applied a seated posture you are not able to maintain stillness for a prolonged period of time. The body is like a child that cannot sit still. It is quite normal for the body to initially create disturbances such as itching, twitching and restless movement. If there are jerks in your body, don't mistakenly think this is because of kundalini awakening. These jerks are obstacles that come because your body is not in the habit of remaining still and they have nothing to do with kundalini. If you practise with patience and persistence for one month you will be able to still your body. Then you will begin to understand there is something very subtle that is responsible for all the movements of your body.

It is not good to sit for meditation if you are very tired or if you have eaten too much. Many of you sit down and sleep comes. Don't force yourself to sit for unnatural lengths of time. As a beginner you should limit the time you sit to fifteen minutes. But those fifteen minutes should be intense.

It is also important not to keep changing your meditation posture. Choose one sitting posture for your meditation, practise it regularly and avoid frequent attempts at new postures. Continual practice of a steady posture will help you to acquire mastery over the body and mind. Fix up a time and place and just sit quietly, nothing more.

In all the meditative postures, do not allow the neck to be twisted or turned to either side, or the head to drop forward, backward or to either side. Release any tension from the neck and shoulders, allowing the shoulders and arms to remain relaxed, with the hands resting on the knees. Touch the thumbs and index fingers in a position called the "finger lock." This is a *mudra* (a particular position of the fingers). It helps to prevent the dissipation of energy.

Now, once you have established a comfortable and steady posture, gently close the eyes and mouth. Mentally survey your body to see that there is no tension in the whole body. Begin from the crown of the head, asking your mind to slowly come down to the feet and then return to the crown, locating any points of tension or other disturbances in the body. Then from the crown of the head come down to your forehead, eyebrows and chin. Systematically move downward from the shoulders, upper arms, forearms, wrists, hands and fingers and then come back up to the shoulders. Shift your focus to the space between the two breasts and on the movement of the abdomen with the breath. Establish serenity in the breath with no shallowness, noise, jerks or pauses. Physical stillness and a serene breath will help you to become aware of the finer forces within.

It is important that you practise at the same time every day. Choose a time that is not inconvenient for your other duties or for other people at home. For one week, practise sitting on a cushion to help you create stillness in the body. You will not immediately become a great yogi or sage just by making the body still, but it's a start. You already know how to move; now you should learn how to sit quietly and be still.

It Is POSSIBLE to Live on Prana Alone

Next is *pranayama*, often referred to as the science of breath. In the context of ashtanga yoga, pranayama practices serve as preparation for pratyahara and dharana. Ultimately, through these practices you can understand the highest source of wisdom, the center of consciousness. This science is vast and recondite and yogis alone know its secrets. Only one who has mastered its practices can understand pranayama, because it must be known experientially. Those who have mastered the profound language of prana are called *pranavedins* (knowers of prana). They do not identify themselves with any sect or religion but accept only the philosophy of prana. They claim their philosophy is so profound, complete and exact that there is no need for any other philosophy or religion. It is a practical philosophy, while other philosophies are based on imagination and speculation. The pranavedins say their philosophy is concrete because they can catch the breath as it flies to where the center of consciousness is hidden. They say they can easily go to that center. To them, all other philosophies, religions and rituals are impractical.

There are very few sages who know this subject, but for those who really know it, pain, misery and even death are nothing. They claim, "We know what death means; we know what birth means. One who knows how to die also knows how to be born." So birth and death are completely under their conscious control. According to the ancient sages, one who knows the science of pranayama knows everything.

I have met a few sages who were masters of pranayama, and I spent many years training with them. They would consciously leave their bodies, and then each of these bodies were declared lifeless after being thoroughly and scientifically examined. Afterward they would come alive again, and their bodies would function as before. In the same manner, they could leave their bodies and get into other bodies and function naturally.

This a very advanced stage, and it is not possible for a common human being to do all this because it requires complete dedication, devotion and self-surrender to the science of pranayama. The pranavedins devote all their time and energy to knowing the kriyas, or methods of the science of prana. They say that because the mind cannot function without the vital force, prana is superior to the functioning of the mind.

Pranayama is one of the most important practices of all forms of yoga. You may not become a pranavedin but through the practice of the basics of pranayama you can change the course of your life. It is a process for isolating the inner self from the influences of worldly thoughts, and a tool that will help you come in touch with the finer forces within. Initially its aim is control over the nervous system, including the autonomic nervous system, leading ultimately to control over prana and the mind. Even though the world has not yet recognized the importance of pranayama, this science is a subtle and complete way to understand and regulate the functioning of the mind and body. The practices of pranayama can help to improve your health, to purify and strengthen the nervous system and can even alleviate a number of diseases ordinarily thought to be incurable. There is no medicine that can substitute for prana. When I was living at my Rishikesh ashram I was made aware of the miraculous nature of prana:

Years ago my Rishikesh ashram was situated very close to the Ganges because at that time there was no barrage. Right in front of my ashram one leper had made a small hut for himself on the banks of the river. The reason he had settled there was to insult me from morning till evening. He omitted no one in his never-ending vocal abuses, including my mother and father. In spite of this, every evening I would go to him to give him milk and to bathe him. This continued for two years until one day a swami from the mountains came. He was a huge man, about six and a half feet tall, totally bald, and was wearing only a loincloth. He marched directly toward me and before he even reached me he angrily asked, "Who is doing all that shouting? It's my meditation time. Tell him to stop."

"If I tell him to stop he will also start to insult you."

Without any hesitation that swami went over to the leper and kicked him hard. There was nothing I could do so I quietly said to him, "That was not a humane thing to do."

He just glared at me and then walked away. I was feeling sorry for the leper because of his condition and because I had been looking after him. But when I went to meet him the next morning, I am giving you living testimony, there was no longer any sign of leprosy on his body! His whole body had healed, and he was completely healthy!

I immediately left to search for that swami. Up to this day I have not been able to find him, though I have tried relentlessly. Although I sent many letters and searched for him throughout the country I was unable to meet him again. I went to another swami who was very aged and asked him if he could give me a similar power so I also could cure lepers with a simple kick. He replied, "One who remains ever with God at the height of ecstasy, automatically acquires all such powers."

I stayed with that swami for some time so he could teach me. Finally I came to the conclusion that human beings have many levels of strength far beyond physical strength. Physical strength is nothing compared to the strength of prana, and the strength of mind is tremendous! You could do wonders in the world, if you just knew the different levels of your own mind — both conscious and unconscious. Jesus Christ had this knowledge and that's how he could change water into wine. You are not aware that you have such a great reservoir within you and so you are suffering.

After I left that swami I started to practise what he had taught me. Wherever I went I used to seek out doctors to show off my newly acquired special ability. I would create a cancerous tumor in my body and then dissolve it in a second's time. I repeated this demonstration many times. But one day it happened that I wasn't able to dissolve a tumor I had created on my bottom. It was troubling me so much I decided to go back to that swami who had taught me all this. Unfortunately he was no longer there. I became more upset and did not know what to do. The tumor was painful, and I knew it was dangerous because it was continuing to grow larger in size and was now about the size of a golf ball. As hard as I tried, I was not able to do anything about it. My method had stopped working.

My master was not there to help me, the swami who had taught me was no longer there, and I did not know anyone else I could approach for help. I knew that if anybody were to come to know of the experiments I had done, they would not believe it. I did not understand what was happening to me, so I started to cry. I quickly decided it was of no use to cry and completed my meditation practice before going to sleep. Just before I fell asleep I heard someone whisper in my ear, "When you wake up, there will be no tumor."

Just as I had been told, the next morning I was tremendously relieved to see that the tumor had disappeared. I do not know how, but it happened.

Pranayama is a vast term and there are several different ways to interpret its meaning, depending on how the word is broken down. The word *prana* means "energy or life force" and *yama* is the control of that energy. The meaning changes if you divide it into the two words *prana* and *ayama*. *Ayama* means "expansion or rising," so another interpretation of the word *pranayama* is "the practice whereby the flow of prana is made more expansive."

Prana is the life force. A subdivision of the word *prana* into two words, gives *pra* and *na*. *Pra* means "first unit of life," that which springs from the source of consciousness, and *na* means "energy." Thus the meaning becomes: The first unit of life expanded to give origin to the manifested universe. And from that first unit of life evolved the mind, the senses and the five gross elements—space, air, fire, water and earth—which support the whole world. Yogis can reverse this process of evolution to return to immortality because they have the power to remain as the mortal self and the immortal both.

Although the real mystery of prana remains veiled, prana comes from the source of consciousness and sustains all life. Prana is the sum total of all energy that is manifest in all living beings and the universe, so there is no qualitative difference between a human being and the universe. The underlying vital principle in both is prana, for there is only one proprietor who is supplying life and breath to everyone without any discrimination. Though you are not aware of it, there is a center within you that is working all the time to supply the life force to you. The first unit of life flows from the center of consciousness to constantly recharge your battery. The One who is supplying prana is the Lord; the one who is receiving it is the soul. This means you are always very close to the reality. All that is present in the world of sense perception, whatever moves or has life, is an expression of prana. Thus you are not just a body, mind and soul; you are also a being of energy.

The force that manifested the universe is called Maha Shakti. *Maha* means "great." The ultimate reality could not manifest itself without this power. According to one of the streams of Indian philosophy the ultimate reality is Maha Shiva or Parama Shiva. The word Shiva in Sanskrit is a combined word: *shava* means "dead body" but the letter "i" makes it Shiva. Without Shakti, Shiva is dead and has no power to manifest anything. Manifestation is the responsibility of Shakti. In individuals, the force that is derived directly from the universal soul, the center of consciousness, is the Kundalini Shakti.

Kundalini is a word that is frequently used but seldom understood. It has a highly secret meaning according to the highest order of yoga and other branches of Indian philosophy and Tibetan and Chinese philosophies. You cannot understand the deeper spiritual aspects of hatha yoga if you do not understand kundalini.

Devatma Shakti is another term used for kundalini. *Deva* means bright being, and *atma* is the soul. *Shakti* means "power," and is the power behind manifestation. There are various levels of powers, and not every power is kundalini. The individual soul or jivatma manifests and functions with the help of Devatma Shakti. Whereas the individual soul has individual Kundalini Shakti, the Cosmic Soul is *Paramatman* (the Absolute Self, Brahman). Qualitatively they are the same, but not quantitatively. As the power to burn cannot be separated from the fire, Shakti cannot be separated from the individual soul.

Kunda means "bowl of fire," or the vessel that contains the fire. The vast reservoir of dormant energy within is called the primal force, or the kundalini. It is the finest form of energy that we have. Only a small part of that energy is needed for the functioning of daily life. If all of the power of kundalini were at your disposal it would not be possible for you to live as a human being.

Kundalini can be known only through direct experience. The ancient yogic manuals contain detailed descriptions of the chakras, which are centers of pranic energy that are represented as lotuses. Each chakra is associated with a certain number of petals, a specific color, a presiding deity and a particular mantra or sound. In the lowest center, the muladhara chakra, is the sleeping serpent-like fire, kundalini, which contains all the latent potential in human beings. It is the aim of yoga to arouse the sleeping kundalini and lead it upward through sushumna, piercing the different chakras, to the sahasrara chakra, the thousand-petalled lotus at the top of the head. This represents the union of the cosmic potential, Shakti, with cosmic consciousness, Shiva. Through this final union the yogi achieves Self-realization and liberation from all bondage. He merges his individual soul, atman, with the Cosmic Soul, Brahman. In order to arouse the latent kundalini energy, one has to practise and perfect asana and pranayama. Some people want to awaken the kundalini because they think they can use that energy for worldly gains and enjoyments. A yogi awakens the kundalini to know the mysteries of the universe.

We are born with a certain amount of prana, which is the active spark of the Kundalini Shakti. The prana that comes from the kundalini maintains the functioning of the entire organism. We also take in prana through the food we eat and the air we breathe. The breath is a gross manifestation of prana. It carries prana in a subtler form than that contained in food and is more indispensable. It is important to remember that prana is not the air or the food itself; they are merely vehicles for this subtle energy. And so it is actually prana, not the breath or food, that is keeping you alive. It is imperative to become aware of your diet and eat nutritious food, but that is not enough. Prana is more important than food. You can live without food for many days but without prana you can live for only a few minutes. However if you know the secrets of the science of pranayama, it is possible to live on prana alone. I have seen yogis who had not taken any food for years, and yet they continued to be very healthy. They could do this because they knew how to utilize the subtle qualities of prana. I have very closely examined the activities of such yogis in the deep Himalayas. You may suspect that they must have been eating something, but when there was nothing around them but snow and a few fir trees, what could they have been eating? They were very happy, their eyes were sparkling and their cheeks remained rosy.

Before undertaking the practices of pranayama it is important to have an understanding of the subtler energy levels. We learned in an earlier chapter that consciousness flows on various degrees and grades to form five koshas or sheaths. The subtlest sheath is anandamaya kosha, the sheath of bliss. Next is vijnanamaya kosha, the buddhi. Less subtle is the mental sheath, manomaya kosha, then comes the pranic or energy sheath, pranamaya kosha, the link between the body and mind. Because of this link, any disturbance in the mind will affect the breath and consequently the body; similarly a disruption in the body and physical functioning will also be experienced in the breath and the mind. The grossest level is the physical body, the annamaya kosha, which is made out of the nutrients obtained from food.

The language of the breath is very profound. The breath is the barometer of the body and mind, and registers any changes that take place in either. If you want to understand your mind, study your breath flow. The breath follows the mind, and the mind follows the breath. Physiological and biological changes occur because of disturbances in your thinking pattern. This is why negative thoughts, uncontrolled thoughts or passive thoughts, can all be injurious. For example, if you are in agony, the breath will become jerky and irregular. Or if somebody gives you some sad news, your breath will become shallow and you may create long pauses. You are not able to control these disturbances because you have lost touch with the autonomic nervous system. But with breathing practices and pranayama you can directly experience and affect the pranic sheath, and consequently gain control of your body and mind.

As mind disturbs the breath, when the body and physical functions are imbalanced, they likewise disturb the breath and the mind. Because of these relationships it is important to have control over the mind and the breath. Regulation of the breath leads to regulation of the mind, and vice versa. If the mind is disturbed there will be a corresponding disturbance in the breath. You can easily observe this in the rapid and irregular breathing of someone who is afraid, excited or overcome by passion. By the same token, continuous regulation of the rhythm of the breath leads to a calm mind. If the breath is harmonious, the mind remains peaceful. We have done many experiments using a breathing apparatus to record the breath pattern during meditation. If you are sitting to meditate but you are thinking about something else, suddenly there will be a jerk in your breath. This proves your thoughts disturb your breath.

The beauty of the Sanksrit language is that one word can have many meanings. For example, in general, *agni* means "fire." But in the Vedas there are more than 300 meanings of agni. The Sanskrit scholar learns how to apply the appropriate meaning accordingly. In aphorism II.53, *dharanasu ca yogyata manasah:* "And (through pranayama) the mind (acquires) fitness for dharana." Patanjali has used the word *dharanasu* or, metaphorically, *dharana-asu.* *Dharana* implies reining in or restraining, and *asu* implies the two horses, or two breaths, inhalation and exhalation. Just as a horse needs a rider, prana is the rider of the breath you are inhaling and exhaling; the breath is the vehicle for prana. If the breath did not have a rider, it would be possible to pump the same composition of air into a dead body and it would come alive again. This cannot happen because prana links the physical and mental life. When this link is broken, death occurs.

The pranic sheath with its individualized characteristic patterns of flow provides the framework around which the structure and functioning of the physical body form themselves. Mastery of the science of pranayama ultimately gives control over the entire pranic sheath or energy body, which leads to control over body and mind. If the vehicle is not right, the driver cannot do anything. Or if the vehicle is in first class condition, but the driver does not know how to drive, it will be chaotic. A yogi is one who has knowledge of both the vehicle and how to drive the vehicle.

You will find many books on the physical body and exercise, on mental life or psychology and on the philosophy and religions of the world. But the topic of prana and the pranic sheath is missing in your educational system. It is prana that feeds and sustains the mind and produces thoughts. All sensations, thinking, feeling and knowing are possible only because of prana. Just as the breath provides a link between body and mind, prana also maintains a link between the unconscious mind and center of consciousness. Prana is therefore related to the mind, through the mind to the will, through the will to the individual soul, atman, and finally to the Cosmic Soul, Brahman.

To appreciate the effects of pranayama, it is helpful to understand the nature and functions of the nervous system because it coordinates the functions of all the other systems in the body. The nervous system is subdivided into the central nervous system and the peripheral nervous system. The central nervous system consists of the brain and the spinal cord, which is an extension of the brain. The peripheral nervous system includes the cranial nerves, spinal nerves and most of the autonomic nervous system. The autonomic nervous system regulates processes in our body that are not normally under our voluntary control, such as the manufacture and release of digestive secretions, heart rate and the regulation of blood pressure, digestion, respiratory rate, salivation, perspiration, urination and sexual arousal. You may understand these functions to a certain extent, but you do not have control over them. Although the autonomic or involuntary system is not normally under voluntary control, if you regularly devote some time for your body, it is possible to bring it under your control.

The autonomic nervous system consists of two complementary systems: the sympathetic and parasympathetic nervous systems. The sympathetic nervous system prepares the body for emergencies and the parasympathetic supports the nurturing functions such as digestion. In some cases the two systems act in opposition on the same organ. For example in the heart, the sympathetic system speeds up the heart rate and increases the strength of contraction, while the parasympathetic slows it down. The most important aspect of the parasympathetic system is the vagus nerve, called the "wandering" nerve because it wanders down from the brain stem to control most of the vital organs in the chest and abdomen. The vagus nerve slows the heartbeat, supervises digestion and brings information to the brain regarding the oxygen and carbon dioxide content of the blood.

There are only two ways to have conscious control over the autonomic nervous system. One is to understand the various vehicles and channels of prana and to practise pranayama or breathing exercises that help to regulate the motion of the lungs; the other way is through the willpower of a one-pointed mind. For thousands of years yogis have known and practised simple breathing exercises that enable control over the heart rate, skin temperature, digestive organs and other functions that were until recently thought to be beyond the control of the conscious mind.

The science of pranayama is intimately connected with the functions of the autonomic nervous system, and its techniques are aimed at bringing these functions under conscious control. This can be achieved by regulating the breath and the motion of the lungs, a vital step in controlling the vagus nerve and the heart rhythm. These in turn bring the autonomic nervous system under voluntary control, thus opening the way to experience the subtler levels of the mind. By controlling the motion of the lungs, you are regulating the exchange that takes place in the storehouse of vital energies. This is the way highly accomplished yogis develop control over the autonomic nervous system.

Even though the ancient yogis did not dissect the human body, their description of the nervous system is consistent with that of modern physiology. The difference is that they did not refer directly to the physical details of the nervous system but to their subtler counterparts. Let us briefly consider the description as given in ancient yogic texts. The texts speak of nadis, or subtle energy channels, and pranas, or vital energies. The physical nerves and impulses are gross manifestations of the subtler nadis and pranas that the yogis discovered many centuries ago. Similarly, the physical plexuses and gland centers represent gross correlates of the chakras that the yogis have also described in great detail. One of the main purposes of the practice of pranayama is to purify the nadis. Once the nadis are purified, pranayama can help to direct the vital forces through these channels and help to bring the mind under volitional control. These practices can reveal a side of life and nature that can be attained in no other way.

According to the ancient yogic texts there are 72,000 nadis, of which three are most significant: ida, pingala and sushumna. In the center, sushumna is related to the spinal cord, and ida and pingala are subtler counterparts of the ganglionated cords of the autonomic nervous system located on either side of the spinal cord. The ida and pingala nadis originate in the muladhara chakra, the subtle equivalent of the pelvic plexus of the sympathetic system, on the left and right side respectively of the *merudanda*, which is a subtle channel that corresponds to the centralis canalis of the spinal cord. The two nadis crisscross each other before they terminate at the nostrils where ida ends in the left nostril and pingala in the right nostril.

The yogic manuals describe ida and pingala as two different flows of energy with distinctive characteristics. You can experiment and confirm these concepts for yourself. If you block your right nostril for one day, you will find that you are feeling depressed. Breathing through the right nostril is used as a therapy for depression. On the other hand, those persons who think about sex all the time are more likely to have a defect in the left nostril. Of course, there could be other reasons also. But in addition to those other reasons, they are predominantly inhaling from their right nostril.

Medical science has not yet completely understood these concepts, but scientists have become aware that inhaling through the right nostril definitely has a different effect than inhaling through the left, and have demonstrated that the electric potentials of the right nostril are different from those of the left nostril. Based on the difference in their effects, yoga refers to the right nostril as the sun, and the left as the moon. By activating one or the other you can compensate heat and coolness in the body respectively. If the right nostril dominates and the breath continuously flows through the right nostril, it will create a different mental state than if the left nostril excessively flows.

Sushumna is centrally located and passes through the merudanda. It also originates at muladhara chakra. As it passes through the merudanda it first pierces the svadhishthana chakra, corresponding to the hypogastric plexus, the manipura chakra, corresponding to the solar plexus, the anahata chakra, corresponding to the cardiac plexus and the vishuddha chakra, corresponding to the pharyngeal plexus. The sushumna then pierces the *talu* (palate), which corresponds to the base of the skull, and divides into an anterior and a posterior portion. The anterior portion proceeds toward the ajna chakra, corresponding to the nasociliary plexus, and joins the *Brahmarandhra,* or cavity of Brahman, which corresponds to the ventricular cavity in the physical body. The posterior portion of the sushumna passes from behind the skull and joins the Brahmarandhra. It is this posterior portion that is developed through pranayama. The realized yogi liberates his soul through the Brahmarandhra.

The ancient yogis also categorized the cosmic prana in the human on the basis of the ten functions it performs. It is through the manifestation of these lesser pranas that all bodily functions are possible and can be coordinated. These are the vehicles that transport and supply the different organs of the body with cosmic energy. Of the ten prana vayus, five are most important: *udana vayu, prana vayu, samana vayu, apana vayu* and *vyana vayu.*

Modern science does not know or recognize the nadis or the vayus.

Vayu means that which flows. It is the agent for all motion, contraction and expansion. Vayu connects all the other forces, making it possible for them to work. Without vayu the tactile sense is inactive as it is vayu that gives us the sensation of touch. The lack of feeling in a paralyzed part is evidence of the absence of vayu. It is the action of vayu that provides the power of digestion and the reduction, absorption and transformation of all food into energy; vayu also eliminates wastes from the body. The nadis are not channels separate from prana; rather they are patterns of the flow of prana. The nadis are weak or strong according to the vayu flowing through them. Where there are disturbances in that flow, where it is overabundant, deficient, distorted, or blocked, these respective disruptions in the field of prana will express in the physical body as excessive growth, congenital anomalies, disease or disorders.

Udana vayu rules the region of the body above the larynx and governs the use of the senses. Prana vayu rules the region between the larynx and the base of the heart and governs the vocal apparatus, the respiratory system and the muscles engaged in breathing. Samana vayu rules in the region between the heart and the navel and governs the metabolic activity involved in digestion. Apana vayu has its abode below the navel and governs the functions of the kidneys, colon, rectum, bladder and genitals. Vyana vayu pervades the whole body and governs the relaxation and contraction of all muscles, voluntary and involuntary, as well as the movement of the joints and the structures around them.

Cosmic energy in the form of prana vayu enters the body through the vehicle of oxygen. Then during inhalation prana takes the form of vyana vayu to reach all the cells of the body and carry away their waste products. During exhalation the force of apana vayu expels the waste products through the vehicle of carbon dioxide. These two vehicles are responsible for cleansing (apana) and nourishing or taking in energy (prana). They hand over their work to the subtle internal vehicles or nadis.

The Kathopanishad describes lower *arani* and upper *arani* – apana and prana vayus. In this context apana is referring to exhalation, and prana to inhalation. Between inhalation and exhalation, and between exhalation and inhalation, you create a pause. If you do not allow a pause, these two aranis will come together and create fire. Prana, or the breath, is a fire.

Death can never come to your door unexpectedly if you know pranayama. With the practice of pranayama not only can you gain control over the pause, but you can also control death. A yogi is one who has perfect control over these pauses. This means he can expand the pause if he wants to do so, to even more than three minutes. Normally if someone does not inhale and exhale for more than three minutes, he will die. There is enough reserve prana in the brain to compensate for the lack of intake for up to three minutes. But after three minutes, only a yogi can survive because he has learned to consciously expand the pause. This is called *bahya kumbhaka,* or suspension of the breath. Such a yogi can maintain this suspension even for six months and during that period remain in a box or somewhere in a cave in a state of samadhi. But this is a rare accomplishment. It may not be possible for you to achieve this, but you can learn to eliminate the pause. A competent and experienced teacher can teach you how to use breathing exercises and pranayama to prolong your life.

Yogis can live for many years because they know how to slow down their metabolism. You can measure the life of a yogi by the number of breaths he takes, whereas a worldly person's life is measured by the number of years he lives. There is a big difference.

If you know the technique you can remain alive even if you take in very little prana, and even though you may appear to be physically and legally dead. On my travels in my youth I came across such a case:

There were two brothers who had somehow learned this technique and turned it into their livelihood. One would pose like a dead man by suspending the breath, while the other announced that his brother had just died. Then a doctor would be called to confirm that he was indeed dead. The other brother would lament to the bystanders that he had no money to cremate his poor brother. He would then collect money from those who felt sorry for him. Every day they moved to a different place and reenacted the same scenario. Once I was in the town where they were playing out their drama. I arrived at the time when the doctor had already pronounced one of the brothers to be dead. I immediately suspected foul play and asked for a thermometer to insert into the rectum. The temperature that registered on the thermometer indicated that he was indeed still alive. As I suspected, they were using a simple technique of suspension of the breath.

Pranayama is a vast term and a complete system that includes the science of breath. The breathing system is different from pranayama. Before undertaking the deeper and subtler practice of pranayama, first you should work with breathing exercises and train your breath.

How the breath behaves is a very interesting subject. In general you commit four gross mistakes when you breathe: shallowness, jerks, noise and pause. If you habitually breathe shallowly, this will eventually cause the rate of the heartbeat to become very fast, which can lead to cardiac arrest. Shallow, fast, jerky or unnatural breathing disturbs the motion of the lungs and also the right vagus nerve. If your breath is noisy, it means there is some blockage in the nose. If you habitually and unconsciously create a pause between the two breaths, you are predisposing yourself to coronary disease, or you may already have certain symptoms of heart disease. That pause is very dangerous and has a destructive effect on the heart. You will find there is some disturbance in the breath or that the breath is irregular in anyone who suffers on account of heart disease. If you are in the habit of breathing unnaturally, you are setting yourself up to have a heart attack, because you are constantly disturbing the pumping station that supplies blood to the brain. You have only two and a half to three minutes reserve oxygen in your brain. If you go beyond this capacity you will suffer from irreversible brain damage or even die. Death literally means to stop breathing. So every time there is a pause in your breath, you are dying. A habitual long pause will lead to death, whereas a short pause will create disease. To omit the pause is yoga.

Once I met a swami who was not a learned man, but had a very special talent. He could predict how long a person was going to live simply by feeling the pulse of that person:

I was very curious about how he was able to do this and asked him what science he was practising. He responded by saying he would give me a book to read and then I should come back the next day.

The name of that book was *Dhuti Vijnanam*. It had been translated from Sanskrit into Hindi. Even though I found it to be a strange book, I felt compelled to read it several times. Three days later I returned the book to him and said, "This is all a hoax. It is of no use to me."

He said, "No, I will prove to you this is all truth. Let's go to the hospital."

He took me to the hospital and introduced me to Dr. Mathro who was a surgeon there. He asked Dr. Mathro's permission to examine the pulse of the patients who were in the hospital.

He replied, "Of course, Swamiji."

The swami went from patient to patient and asked each one to lie down and then examined the pulse. He predicted when each patient was going to die and afterwards said that none of them would live more than two years. He could do this because he had knowledge of the pause. His method was very scientific and he explained the mathematics of it to me.

A little pause is natural, but if that little pause expands, you will create some disease. Try to omit the pause as much as you can, and you will remain healthy.

Yogic science says you can control your breath by controlling the motion of your lungs. To regulate the motion of the lungs means to regulate the input of oxygen and the output of carbon dioxide. For that purpose you have to do certain exercises. The first is to maintain balance between exhalation and inhalation. If exhalation is incomplete, not only will toxins accumulate in your body and create many problems, your thinking will always be clouded. Poor breathing habits are prominent among the reasons that many people find it difficult to concentrate.

By doing breathing exercises you can regulate all four of the common disturbances in the breath. Breathing exercises directly affect the motion of the lungs, even though respiration is generally considered to be under involuntary control. Exhalation and inhalation are like two guards who are guarding the city of life. They have a very important duty to perform and you can train them to do it properly. If you know how to control these guards, the city of life remains protected. Otherwise you are vulnerable to attack by external and internal negative forces.

The first step in the practical aspects of the science of breath is breath awareness. Breath awareness involves developing awareness of the qualities of your breath simply by observing it. When you pay attention towards your breath, just feel the flow of it. Don't try to visualize anything or have preconceived ideas about what you are going to experience, because you should be freely exploring. The practice of breath awareness can help you to decrease and ultimately eliminate the pause. Even if you have heart disease, nothing will happen if you learn to decrease the pause and do not breathe shallowly. I know someone who has a hole in one of the chambers of the heart by birth. He did not find out about this condition until the age of fifty-six. He had been practicing meditation under the guidance of my master for many years, so when he found out about his condition he immediately consulted my master. My master taught him some breathing practices to do and later I also taught him something. Now he is in his eighties and is very healthy, even though he still has a peanut-like hole in the third chamber of his heart.

Once you are aware of the qualities of your breath that need to be changed, the next important exercise is deep diaphragmatic breathing. The simple practice of deep breathing through diaphragmatic movement is the foundation of the science of breath. In essence, control of the diaphragm is the basis of all breathing exercises. It is the action of the diaphragm that is responsible for drawing air into the lungs and expelling air from the lungs. Therefore it is necessary that all students of yoga comprehend the function of the diaphragm.

The lungs are situated on each side of the chest, with the heart, great vessels and esophagus separating the lungs and the air passages leading to them. At the base of the lungs is the diaphragm, the muscular wall that divides the chest cavity from the abdomen. The diaphragm is the strongest muscle in the body. Even in an otherwise weak person, the diaphragm is very strong. But if it is not used, like any other muscle, the diaphragm will lose that strength. When you push in the abdomen with exhalation, the abdomen in turn pushes against the diaphragm. Subsequently the diaphragm contracts and pushes against the lungs. This helps the lungs to expel carbon dioxide. At the end of exhalation, the diaphragm relaxes, allowing the lungs to expand and create more space for the intake of oxygen.

To learn diaphragmatic breathing it is best to use *makarasana*, the crocodile pose. This pose is helpful in the beginning because in this posture it is easy to observe the movement of the abdomen with the breath. Also it helps to maintain stillness of the chest so it does not become involved in the breathing process. If you practise five minutes at a time, three times a day, it will help you. When you feel you have gained some control and understanding of the breath, you can then lie on your back in *shavasana* (the corpse pose), to practise. With diligent, conscientious effort, you can form the habit of breathing diaphragmatically in one month's time. Once it becomes a habit, you will remain very healthy.

To breathe diaphragmatically you have to observe the four basic qualities: first, do not breathe shallowly. You should fill the lungs with each breath. If you habitually breathe deeply you will increase your lung capacity, and it will keep increasing with continued practice. Next, do not allow a long pause between the two breaths. The third thing to notice is the quality of the flow of the breath.

The breath should be smooth without any jerks. If the breath flows smoothly, relaxation occurs; if the breath is irregular, it is very difficult to rest. Lastly, the breath should be silent. Noisy breathing is a sign of obstruction in the nostrils. If the nostrils are chronically obstructed, you will have to inhale through the mouth, which is an unhealthy practice in general.

While you are doing breathing exercises, you have to give the mind something to do, or it will keep running here and there. One way to keep the mind busy is to follow the flow of the breath with the mind. The breath will then follow the mind. A simple exercise is the following: Exhale as though you are exhaling from the crown of the head down to the toes and then inhale from the toes back up to the crown of the head. If you develop the habit of paying attention to the breath, mind will be conscious of the breath's presence, and the breath will be conscious of the mind's presence. Another option is to concentrate on a sound, as long it does not disturb your breath.

In the initial stages of the practice of diaphragmatic breathing it is best to establish even breathing, in which the length of inhalation equals that of exhalation. The next phase is the practice of 2 to 1 breathing, one of the best of all breathing exercises in which the exhalation is twice as long as the inhalation. The prolonged exhalation augments the process of releasing toxins and carbon dioxide. If you live in a modern polluted city, this practice can help you to remain free of toxins. Begin by inhaling to the count of four and then exhaling to the count of eight. Initially you can use counting so you come to know what your capacity is. Once you know your capacity, it is better to leave the counting, even in the mind, because it will create jerks in the breath, which is very bad for the heart.

A better way to measure your breath is to practise in the following way: Inhale as though you are inhaling from the root of the spinal column to the crown of your head, mentally repeating the sound "*so.*" Then exhale as though you are exhaling from the crown of your head to your toes along with the sound "*hum.*" When you breathe in this manner, the exhalation will automatically be twice as long as inhalation and there will be no need to count. Gradually you can increase the count according to your capacity. Once you are able to do a count of 20 : 40, you can work up to the highest count of 30 : 60, which is considered to be the finest among all the breathing exercises.

Do not rush to increase the count. Take at least six months to practise this exercise. Then you will find that your body has become very smooth like silk due to a hormonal change that has taken place in the body. Sometimes the male hormone disturbs the female body, and the female body starts to grow hair where it is not needed, such as on the face. Regular practise of this 2 to 1 breathing exercise can prevent this from happening. It is advisable for women who have gone through a hysterectomy or who are menopausal or post-menopausal to practise this for harmonious hormonal balance.

After practising even diaphragmatic breathing, repeat 2 to 1 breathing ten times, followed by even breathing again. Whatever breathing exercises you do, you should complete your practice with even breathing. Practise three times a day, doing three sets at a time. In a few days time you will find your breath has become calmer, smoother and quieter. These breathing exercises are very therapeutic. Those who practise them will never have a heart attack. They can give heart attacks to others, but not to themselves!

There are many other breathing exercises that have specific effects on your health and spiritual growth. In the advanced stages you can do those breathing exercises that are more difficult and also begin to practise pranayama. If you decide to practise pranayama you must take into consideration your lifestyle, the kind of food you eat, the atmosphere you breathe and your mental attitude. There is a saying: *He who fasts and he who eats too much; he who does not sleep and he who sleeps too much; he who works too much and he who does not work; none of these can be adepts.* Practise in a quiet isolated place with clean air. Always be aware of your physical capacity and strength, never forcing yourself beyond your comfortable limits. It is better to gradually increase the length of your practice in small stages.

In the beginning practices of pranayama the breath has three phases: *puraka, kumbhaka* and *rechaka* – inhalation, retention and exhalation respectively. Basic pranayama involves the regulation of these three phases. It is the practice of inhaling to one's capacity, suspending the breath as long as possible, and exhaling until the lungs are as empty as possible, without using force or undue restraint. Like all advanced breathing and pranayama practices, you should learn kumbhaka under the guidance of a competent teacher. If you retain oxygen after inhalation and do not allow your lungs to exhale immediately, the cells will start to absorb and consume the reserves within. You can do this under your control. In this practice you inhale, retain and exhale in the proportion of 1:4:8.

Patanjali conveys the importance of pranayama in aphorisms II.49, II.50 and II.51. The result of the practice of pranayama is given in aphorism II.52: *tatah ksiyate prakasavaranam:* (Then the cloud of darkness that obscures the light melts away). The light is ever present but you do not see it because the cloud of ignorance is obscuring the view. With the practice of pranayama that cloud melts away and you can clearly see the light in all its brilliance.

Pranayama is a preparation for the higher rungs of ashtanga yoga. It is difficult to train the mind if the body and the breath create obstacles for you. Breathing exercises and pranayama help to lead the sadhaka to the deeper stages of pratyahara and dharana.

The Major SOURCE of Disturbances

Is WITHIN

Pratyahara is withdrawal of the senses from the objects of the external world. This is a voluntary mental process. It does not mean to withdraw from the world or from your relationships, family or duties. The senses are the greatest source of distraction for your mind. They create obstacles for you and do not allow you to sit quietly. It may seem that the senses are contacting the objects of the world, but actually the mind uses the five senses of sight, hearing, touch, taste and smell to contact those objects. If you do not allow the mind to use the senses, the senses cannot take in the objects in the external world, because the senses are totally dependent on the mind. As soon as the mind becomes active on waking from sleep, the senses are simultaneously activated. The mind is thus constantly bombarded and dissipated by the myriad of sensations from the external world. The purpose of the practice of pratyahara is to protect the mind from the distractions of the senses. By consciously not allowing the senses to contact the objects of the world, you are suspending the otherwise endless onslaught of fresh impressions that disturb the mind and get stored in the unconscious.

It will take a lot of determination, practice and discipline to be able to voluntarily withdraw your mind from the senses, but it is possible. However, even though with pratyahara you can eradicate the onslaught of external distractions, impressions can still come from the unconscious. You have stored millions of impressions of your daily life and previous lives within the bed of memory of your unconscious mind, and they are lying on many levels. These impressions are of two types: *klishta* and *aklishta* — pleasant and unpleasant. Some are dormant, some you can observe and analyze and some you cannot analyze because they are deeply embedded in the unconscious, and you have forgotten them. So you may be successful at pratyahara, but your concentration can still be disturbed by the impressions coming forward from the unconscious. When the senses are withdrawn, those impressions will immediately start to surface to the conscious mind. Why? If you catch hold of my right hand and try to fight with me or hurt me, what will happen? Automatically my left hand will come into action to protect me. In the same manner, when you try to control any part of the conscious mind, the totality of mind becomes active. Because of the sheer vastness of the unconscious mind, it is exceedingly more difficult to control. It is like trying to control an elephant by catching its tail. The elephant will definitely throw you away. Whenever the mind becomes a little bit free, memories of the past surface. For example, if you withdraw your mind from the sense of sight by closing your eyes, you will find that if mind does not have something else to concentrate upon, it will immediately start to recall previous experiences. This is why besides withdrawing the mind from the senses, you will also have to have an object on which the mind can focus.

The best way to deal with the impressions surfacing from the unconscious is to decide that no matter what comes in your mind, you will not get involved with it. Don't fight with yourself. Tell yourself to let go of whatever comes, no matter what happens: *I have controlled my senses and I am not going to allow my mind to run outwardly. My posture is still and my breath is harmonious. I will not allow anything that comes in my mind during meditation to sway me. Whatever comes, I will let go of it.*

An intermediate step of pratyahara is when you have withdrawn your awareness from external objects, but still you are aware of yourself as having shape and form. One day you will have to go beyond that also. Some persons who meditate can consciously free themselves from the physical body and observe themselves from the viewpoint of an external witness. But that is not a very safe way except for trained yogis who use the energy body to travel by consciousness separate from the physical body. It is more helpful to affirm in silence: *I have no body, no breath, no senses, no mind; I am pure Atman, established in peace, bliss and happiness.* Both methods are used; the latter is higher than the former.

It will not be possible for you to concentrate, meditate and then to attain samadhi if you do not practise voluntary withdrawal of the senses from the objects of the world. Withdrawal of the senses will help you to voluntarily isolate your mind and prepare you for the next step. To perfect pratyahara you have to have profound knowledge of the totality of your mind and internal states. Whenever you want to withdraw your mind from the external world, you should be able to do it. The mind and senses should be under your control. Presently your mind is not fit for concentration or attention. Pratyahara is necessary to achieve tranquility and is preliminary to concentration. With the help of voluntary withdrawal of the senses, the mind will no longer be distracted and you will be able to concentrate. It is therefore important that the student of yoga acquire the ability to voluntarily draw the senses inward. You have to prepare the mind for meditation by developing perfect control over the senses.

Pratyahara is a preliminary practice in the process of learning to meditate. Once you know how to arrest all the senses, it will become easier for you to meditate. There are many methods of meditation, but the finest method is *sukhamana sushumna*, in which the practitioner elevates the mind to a state of joy in which it is not distracted or dissipated.

When you sit to meditate first become aware of the surrounding space, withdrawing your attention from the past and the future in order to experience the present moment more completely. Then mentally affirm, *I am not the body, I am not the breath, I am not the senses, I am not the mind. These are all my instruments. The mind is my subtler instrument. I am Atman, the Infinite.* During this process every time the mind wanders outward, you should gently draw it inward. To be successful at this practice, you have to develop two qualities — determination and power of concentration: *Now I am meditating. No power on earth, whether external or internal, will have the power to disturb me.*

In this volume it has been explained that disturbances coming from the external world can be curtailed by practicing the five external steps of ashtanga yoga. Yoga science is divided into two parts, external and internal, because there are conflicts within and without. If you can get rid of all conflicts you will understand your external and internal being and the whole science of life.

The first five steps of ashtanga yoga: yama, niyama, asana, pranayama and pratyahara, constitute the outer face of yoga. The more you understand the functions of the mind, the more aware you will be that it is your mind that is creating disturbances for you. Disturbances do not come from outside; the major source of disturbances is within. By practicing the first five steps of ashtanga yoga you can gain conscious control over your mind and your external activities.

The next three steps—dharana, dhyana and samadhi—are internal techniques for having control over mind and its modifications. These three steps will be discussed in the next volume. Then you will learn how to deal with internal disturbances, which are deeper and stronger than the distractions of the external world. If you can do that, you can have perfect control over yourself. Without conscious effort, you cannot have control over your mind. Control is not something that hurts you; control gives you the power to understand things properly. You become master when you control something. Otherwise, things will start to control you.

Ashtanga yoga is like a ladder with eight steps. You climb the rungs one by one until finally you reach the top. Gradually start to work with yourself, step by step. This path can help you to become aware of the center of reality. Before you can experience samadhi, the highest state of yoga, you have to practise these basics. It is in your hands to enlighten yourself. You have the potential, but you tend to become discouraged and give up shortly after you start something. If you are determined and you persist, you will definitely benefit. The center of reality is very close and near to you. The more you become aware of this, the closer you will be to enlightenment. The aim of ashtanga yoga is to lead you to samadhi, the height of perfection.

Never stop working with yourself. All the methods of yoga have ethical and moral perfection as their basis, and thus a new world order of love could easily be achieved by the universal adoption of even the simplest and most fundamental observances of yogic discipline.

Glossary

Abhnivesha: Strong desire for life and abject fear of death. See *kleshas.*

Ahamkara: see *antahkarana.*

Ahimsa: Nonharming. See *yamas.*

Antahkarana: Inner instrument, the mind. It has four constituents: *buddhi,* which discriminates and decides; *ahamkara*, literally the I-maker, the feeling of *I* and *mine*; *chitta*, the unconscious mind, the store of impressions; and *manas*, which gathers information from the senses to present to buddhi.

Aparigraha: Nonpossessiveness. See *yamas.*

Asanas: In Patanjali, the sitting postures appropriate for meditation.

Ashtanga yoga: Eight-limbed yoga; the eight independent and sequential limbs or rungs of yoga. The first five steps constitute the outer face: *yama, niyama, asana, pranayama,* and *pratyahara;* the next three steps are internal: *dharana, dhyana* and *samadhi.* See also *yamas* and *niyamas.*

Asmita: Egotism or self-centeredness. See *kleshas.*

Asteya: Nonstealing. See *yamas.*

Atman: 1. Pure consciousness, the Self. 2. Oneself, the lower self (atman).

Avidya: Ignorance or lack of awareness of the ultimate reality. See *kleshas.*

Brahmacharya: Conserving and utilizing energy. See *yamas.*

Brahman: The Self, the absolute reality, whose nature is sat-chit-ananda (truth, consciousness and bliss).

Buddhi: Intellect; that faculty of mind which discriminates and decides. See *antahkarana.*

Chakra: Center of consciousness.

Chitta: 1. The storehouse of past impressions. See *antahkarana.* 2. The totality of the mind.

Dharana: Concentration. See *ashtanga yoga.*

Dhyana: Meditation. See *ashtanga yoga.*

Duhkha: Pain, worry, misery, suffering.

Dvesha: Repulsion. See *kleshas* .

Gunas: Qualities; especially the three qualities of the mind: *sattva* (tranquil, peaceful); *rajas* (active); and *tamas* (inert, dull, dark).

Ishvara pranidhana: Surrender to God or the ultimate reality. See *niyamas.*

Jiva: The individual soul when it mistakenly considers itself to be limited.

Jnana: Knowledge.

Karma: Action.

Khechari mudra: An advanced yoga practice.

Kleshas: The five afflictions: **avidya** (ignorance or lack of awareness of the reality); *asmita* (egotism or self-centeredness); *raga* (attachment towards the things of the world); *dvesha* (repulsion); *abhinivesha* (strong desire for life and abject fear of death).

Koshas: External coverings of the Atman within. They are five: *annamaya kosha* (the physical body); *pranamaya kosha* (the pranic or energy sheath); *manomaya kosha* (the mental sheath); *vijnanamaya kosha* (the buddhi); and *anandamaya kosha* (the sheath of bliss).

Kriya yoga: Practical preliminary yoga comprising *tapas* (knowing how to control the senses); *svadhyaya* (self-study; the study of one's own nature): and *ishvara pranidhana* (self-surrender).

Kundalini: The dormant energy in the muladhara chakra at the base of the spine.

Manas: 1. The faculty of mind that gathers information from the senses and presents it to buddhi. See *antahkarana*. 2. The totality of the mind.

Maya: Apparent reality; that which appears to exist but which does not exist.

Moksha: Liberation; final emancipation from all the kleshas, all pain and suffering.

Nadi: A channel for prana.

Nishedha: A prohibition; e.g. a-steya, do not steal.

Niyamas: The five observances, which are moral commitments: *shaucha* (cleanliness within and without); *santosha* (contentment); *tapas* (austerity or control of the senses); *svadhyaya* (self-study and study of the scriptures); *ishvara pranidhana* (surrender to God, the ultimate reality.

Prakriti: Elemental matter.

Prana: The life force.

Pranayama: Control of energy or life force.

Pratyahara: Conscious withdrawal of the senses from the objects of the external world.

Purusha: 1. Cosmic consciousness. 2. The individual consciousness that sees through prakriti.

Raga: Attachment towards the objects of the world. See *kleshas*.

Raja Yoga: Royal yoga; Swami Vivekananda's term for ashtanga yoga.

Rajas: The active quality of mind. See *gunas*.

Sadhaka: One who engages in sadhana, spiritual practice.

Sadhana: Spiritual practice.

Sadhana Pada: The second of the four padas, or sections, of the Yoga Sutras. The foundation of spiritual practice.

Samadhi: Establishment in one's essential nature.

Samskaras: Impressions and strong motivations carried from the past or previous lifetimes.

Sankalpa shakti: Determination.

Santosha: Contentment. See *niyamas.*

Sat, chit, ananda: Truth, consciousness, bliss. See *Brahman.*

Sattva: The tranquil, peaceful quality of mind. See *gunas.*

Satya: Truth. See *yamas.*

Shakti: In tantric literature, the female principle of life.

Shaucha: Cleanliness within and without. See *niyamas.*

Shiva: In tantric literature, the male principle of life.

Siddhi: 1. Proficiency, success. 2. A supernatural power that may arise on the path of spirituality that can become an obstacle for the aspirant.

Sukha: Easy, pleasant, comfortable.

Svadhyaya: Self-study, which includes the study of the scriptures and the lives of great people. See *niyamas.*

Tamas: The quality of inertia. See *gunas.*

Tapas: Control of the senses. See *niyamas.*

Vijnana: The method used to receive knowledge.

Vrittis: Modifications of the mind.

Yamas: Restraints; also moral commitments. They are: *ahimsa* (noninjuring); *satya* (truth); *asteya* (nonstealing); *brahmacharya* (conserving and utilizing energy); and *aparigraha* (nonpossessiveness).

Yoga: Union with the Universal Self.

Index

About the Author

Swami Rama was born in the Himalayas and was initiated by his master into many yogic practices. His master also sent him to other yogis and adepts of the Himalayas to gain new perspectives and insights into the ancient teachings. At the young age of twenty-four he was installed as Shankaracharya of Karvirpitham in South India. Swamiji relinquished this position to pursue intense sadhana in the caves of the Himalayas. Having successfully completed this sadhana, he was directed by his master to go to Japan and to the West in order to illustrate the scientific basis of the ancient yogic practices. At the Menninger Foundation in Topeka, Kansas, Swamiji convincingly demonstrated the capacity of the mind to control so-called involuntary physiological processes such as the heart rate, temperature, and brain waves. Swamiji's work in the United States continued for twenty-three years, and in this period he established the Himalayan International Institute.

Swamiji became well known in the United States as a yogi, teacher, philosopher, poet, humanist, and philanthropist. His models of preventive medicine, holistic health, and stress management have permeated the mainstream of western medicine. In 1993 Swamiji

295

returned to India where he established the Himalayan Institute Hospital Trust in the foothills of the Garhwal Himalayas. Swamiji left this physical plane in November, 1996, but the seeds he has sown continue to sprout, bloom, and bear fruit. His teachings, embodied in the words, "Love, Serve, Remember," continue to inspire the many students whose good fortune it was to come in contact with such an accomplished, selfless, and loving master.

Himalayan Institute Hospital Trust

The Himalayan Institute Hospital Trust (HIHT) was conceived, designed, and orchestrated by Dr. Swami Rama, with the mission of developing integrated and cost-effective approaches to health care, education and economic development for under-served populations worldwide. Swamiji established the Himalayan Institute Hospital Trust in 1989 starting with an outpatient clinic of only two rooms. Today, nestled in the foothills of the Himalayas, we have a beautiful 200-acre campus housing an ultra-modern 750-bed multi-specialty hospital, the Rural Development Institute (RDI), the Swami Rama Himalayan University (SRHU), an Ayurveda Centre, and a Cancer Research Institute (CRI).

The Himalayan Hospital is serving approximately 10 million people of Garhwal, and adjoining areas. The hospital includes a comprehensive Reference Laboratory, state-of-the-art Radiology Department, 24-hour Emergency Department, well-equipped Intensive Care Unit, Blood Bank, Eye Bank, modern Dialysis Unit, Cardiac Care Unit and Cath Lab. CRI addresses all aspects of cancer control and cancer therapy supported by research and education. Through well-equipped mobile vans, the hospital also provides health care services to communities in difficult to reach areas.

In order to improve the quality of life of the rural population of Uttarakhand and adjoining areas, RDI is actively engaged in healthcare, education, skill development, adolescent awareness programs, income generation activities, main-streaming of the differently-abled, water and sanitation programs, and relief and rehabilitation measures.

Swami Rama Himalayan University (SRHU), a State University was established vide Uttarakhand Act No. 12 of 2013. The constituent colleges of SRHU are the Himalayan Institute of Medical Sciences, Himalayan College of Nursing, Himalayan School of Management Studies offering both undergraduate and post graduate programs, and Himalayan School of Engineering and Technology offering undergraduate courses in Civil, Mechanical and Electrical Engineering, Electronics and Communication, and Computer Sciences.

SRHU also offers Ph.D. program in various specialties. The Himalayan Institute of Medical Sciences runs undergraduate (M.B.B.S.) and postgraduate courses (M.D./M.S. and Diploma) in 18 disciplines. as well as paramedical degree courses in several disciplines. The Himalayan College of Nursing offers a 4-year B.Sc., a 3-year GNM diploma, a 2-year Post-Basic B.Sc. and M.Sc. programs. Nursing students are also introduced to the basics of alternate systems of health care including yoga science.

HIHT has established outpatient and inpatient therapeutic programs of Homeopathy, Osteopathy, Ayurveda, Yoga and Holistic Medicine. The Ayurveda Centre offers a comprehensive panchakarma program for detoxification, rejuvenation, and treatment of chronic diseases. In 1997, the Swami Rama Centre was created to ensure that the words and works of Swmai Rama continue to be available as a source of inspiration to countless spiritual seekers. The center also continues to publish new books, CDs, and videos incorporating Swami Rama's teachings.

For information contact: Himalayan Institute Hospital Trust, Swami Ram Nagar, P.O. Jolly Grant, Dehradun 248016, Uttarakhand, India, 91-135-247-1200, pb@hihtindia.org, www. hihtindia.org

Swami Rama Society, Inc.

The Swami Rama Society is a registered, nonprofit, tax-exempt organization committed to Swami Rama's vision of bridging the gap between Western science and Eastern wisdom. The Society was established to provide financial assistance and technical support to institutions and individuals who are ready to implement this vision in the U.S.A. and abroad.

For information contact:
Swami Rama Society, Inc.
5000 W. Vliet St.
Milwaukee, WI 53211 U.S.A.
414-454-0500
info@swamiramasociety.org
www.swamiramasociety.org

Samadhi the Highest State of Wisdom
Yoga the Sacred Science, volume one
Swami Rama
ISBN 978-81-88157-01-3, $14.95, paperback, 256 pages

OM the Eternal Witness
Secrets of the Mandukya Upanishad
Swami Rama
ISBN 978-81-88157-43-3, $14.95, paperback, 202 pages

Sacred Journey
Living Purposefully and Dying Gracefully
Swami Rama
ISBN 978-81-88157-00-6, $12.95, paperback, 136 pages

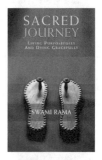

The Essence of Spiritual Life
A Companion Guide for the Seeker
Swami Rama
ISBN 978-190100-49-6, $12.95, paperback, 136 pages

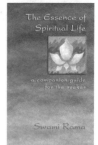

Distributed in U.S.A. by Lotus Press,
PO Box 325, Twin Lakes, WI 53181 U.S.A., www.lotuspress.com. Order toll free at 1-800-824-6396, lotuspress@lotuspress.com

At the Feet of a Himalayan Master

Remembering Swami Rama
Volume One
ISBN 978-81-88157-62-4, $16.98,
paperback, 344 pages

At the Feet of a Himalayan Master

Remembering Swami Rama
Volume Two
ISBN 978-81-88157-66-2, $18.98,
paperback, 304 pages

Conscious Living

A Guidebook for Spiritual Transformation
Swami Rama
ISBN 978-188157-03-7, $12.95,
paperback, 160 pages

Let the Bud of Life Bloom

A Guide to Raising Happy and Healthy Children
Swami Rama
ISBN 978-188157-04-4, $12.95,
paperback, 102 pages

Distributed in U.S.A. by Lotus Press,
PO Box 325, Twin Lakes, WI 53181 U.S.A.,
www.lotuspress.com. Order toll free at
1-800-824-6396, lotuspress@lotuspress.com